C00A174976

To
CHERNOBYL,
with love

Jim Gillies
with
Murray Scougall

To May + Pete
best wishes
Jim

Published by Jim Gillies with the assistance of Waverley Books Ltd.

First published 2011.

© 2011 Jim Gilles and Murray Scougall

A catalogue entry for this book is available from the British Library.

ISBN 978-1-84934-188-2

Printed and bound in the EU.

Contents

Foreword

It was in 1999 that Jim Gillies visited our town for the first time.

An electrical engineer from Scotland, he had collected money to help Ukrainian children. What motivated this unassuming man who was no longer a youngster? What made him take this brave step and go on a long journey to bring aid to Ukrainian children?

He is simply a man of a big heart and a sensitive soul...

I find no words adequate enough to express my gratitude, and the gratitude of the personnel of the children's ward and of the children themselves, for his good works on our behalf.

Since then Jim has visited our ward almost yearly.

Medicines, medical equipment, linen, furniture, bedding, white goods, household utensils, radio and television equipment... practically more than half of what we need has been purchased thanks to the funds provided by Jim Gillies.

Each autumn we eagerly wait for his visit. We see the results of his assistance at every step, while the State remains indifferent to our problems.

Today Jim Gillies is a retired man, but his eagerness to ease the lot of the child victims of the Chernobyl disaster grows by the year.

We wish Jim and his family all the best and many successes in his noble but hard work.

Dr Victoria Baklanova

Introduction

On the morning of April 28, 1986 radiation was detected on the clothing of workers at Forsmark Nuclear Power Plant in Sweden. It was immediately feared that there was a leak but tests showed the plant to be clear. So where was it coming from?

Scientists at a laboratory in Studvik, on Sweden's Baltic Coast, had also picked up on the high radiation levels. At first they believed it must be a problem with one of their own country's power plants, but thanks to wind data and technical assistance from American scientists, by the afternoon they had traced the radioactivity seven hundred miles away to the Soviet Union. The Swedish government went to their Soviet counterparts and presented their case and demanded information.

It was only then that the world learned of the most catastrophic nuclear accident ever to have happened. An explosion that is recognised by just one word.

Chernobyl.

At 1.23am on April 26, the one thousand tonne lid was blown off of Reactor 4 at the Chernobyl Nuclear Power Plant in Ukraine after a planned safety test experiment went horribly wrong. Horrendously poisonous plumes of radiation swept over the Soviet states and the fallout drifted across large parts of Europe and contaminated the land.

The discovery by the Swedes forced the Soviet authorities to not just admit the accident to the world, but also forced them to tell their own people just how serious the explosion really was. Prior to the Swedish detection, a specially formed government committee had been created to deal with the accident. But its remit seemed to be to organise a cover up, rather than tell the truth.

The committee arrived in Chernobyl on the evening of the 26th, by which point two people were already dead and fifty-two were in hospital. Overnight, a full day after the devastation was triggered, the government team decided to acknowledge the destruction of the reactor and to evacuate Pripyat, the town built especially to house the power plant workers.

The following message was played on local media, "An accident has occurred at the Chernobyl Nuclear Power Plant. One of the atomic reactors has been damaged. Measures are being taken to eliminate the consequences of the accident. Aid will be given to those affected and a committee of government inquiry has been set up."

At first, that was all of the information forthcoming so people carried on with their lives as usual. Workers went to their jobs, including the power plant despite its state, children played freely and women hung out washing. But word quickly spread of the condition of the firemen who were immediately on the scene at the power plant's "fire", iodine tablets were being handed out to children, and police were telling residents to stay indoors with the windows shut.

But why?

At 2pm on April 27th, the mass evacuation of a town with a population of fifty thousand began. As its residents piled onto buses they were told it was only a temporary measure, probably just three days, in a cynical move designed to reduce panic and baggage. A town was emptied because of the greatest industrial disaster in the history of mankind, yet the rest of the world knew nothing about either event. But perhaps the Soviet authorities failed to recognise that the explosion was the one thing that even they would find impossible to oppress, as one hundred and ninety tonnes of toxic materials expelled into the atmosphere and rose to an altitude in excess of twelve hundred metres.

Traces of radiation substances were eventually found as far away as North America and Japan, although only in very small quantities. But the toxicity lingered. Indeed, it was only in July 2010 that Scottish sheep farms were finally deemed to be clear from the Chernobyl fallout. However, three hundred and thirty farms in North Wales and eight in Cumbria remain under restrictions.

The most contaminated territories lie in the north of Ukraine, the south and east of Belarus and the western border area between Belarus and Russia. At the time, seven million people, including three million kids, lived in these parts. The affected territories were split into four different zones of contamination in Ukraine and Russia, five in Belarus. In Ukraine these are called The Exclusion Zone, Zone of Obligatory Resettlement, Zone of Guaranteed Resettlement and zone four is known as the Zone of Enhanced Radiological Control. Today five-and-a-half million people, including one million kids, still live in the contaminated territories.

Health impacts in the aftermath are extensive. They include

thyroid cancer in children, leukaemia, nervous system disorders, tumours, birth defects, cardiac abnormalities, bone and muscle disorders, diabetes, cardiovascular diseases and genetic mutations.

So what led to the explosion that has resulted in twenty-five years of illness, suffering, displacement, poverty and death?

The Chernobyl Nuclear Power Plant had been operating since 1977 and reactor 4 was in service from 1983. An experiment was scheduled in reactor 4 on April 25th, 1986 to test whether the turbines could produce sufficient energy to keep the coolant pumps running in the event of a loss of power until the emergency diesel generator was activated. In order to allow the test run to go uninterrupted the safety systems had to be turned off.

The test was supposed to conclude during the day shift, where the workers had been told in advance about the trial and knew the procedures. As planned, there was a gradual reduction in the output of power and by the start of the day shift the output was down to fifty per cent of its nominal 3200MW thermal. But another regional power station went offline unexpectedly, prompting Kiev's electrical grid controller to request the test be postponed because Chernobyl's power was needed for the peak evening time.

At 11.04pm, the Kiev grid controller gave the go ahead for the test to resume. By now, though, it was the night shift that were on duty. The one hundred and sixty workers had little time to prepare for the experiment, they hadn't been briefed and they hadn't expected to participate in the test before arriving for work that evening. There were a further three hundred workers at the building site of reactors 5 and 6.

The control rods – which regulate the fission process in a nuclear reactor to slow the chain reaction – were lowered to reduce the output to twenty per cent of its normal power. The fewer control rods that are positioned between the fuel elements, the greater the reactor power. But this process was flawed in the Chernobyl reactors' design. In this case, if the rods were raised and then lowered between the elements, the initial effect was the opposite of that which was expected – the power actually increased. But of course this wasn't known as April 25th turned into April 26th.

And Leonid Toptunov, the operator responsible that night for the reactor's operational regime, including movement of those control rods, certainly didn't know about it. He was a young engineer who had worked independently as a senior engineer for just three months.

Power was supposed to be reduced to 700 – 1000 MW thermal. This was reached at 00.05 but it continued to decrease. When it dropped to 500MW, Toptunov reinserted the control rods. But he pushed in too many of them at once and too far, bringing the reactor to a near shutdown with just one per cent of power at 30MW.

The control room engineers decided to raise the rods to increase the output. But by 1am the power was still only at seven per cent, so they raised more rods and continued to do so until power rose to 12 per cent.

At that time, 1.23am, the test was started. But within seconds the power surged to dangerously high levels. The emergency shutdown button was pressed but with the power one hundred times higher than normal, it failed to work.

The reactor overheated. The water coolant steamed. The fuel

pellets began to explode in the core. Two explosions occurred one after the other, blowing the domed roof off. The burning contents inside erupted towards the night sky, like a malevolent fountain tapped straight out of hell.

It took only seconds, but in that moment millions of people's lives changed completely and one of the world's worst disasters was instantly etched into the annals of history.

Around four hundred times more radioactive material was released from the burning reactor than during the atomic bombing of Hiroshima.

At 1.26am the fire alarm was activated and two minutes later the first firefighters arrived on the scene. It's rumoured the Chernobyl Power Station Firefighter Brigade didn't know or weren't warned of the high level of radioactivity at the burning blaze.

Radiation levels in the worst affected areas of the reactor were estimated at 5.6 roentgens per second, which is more than 20,000 roentgens per hour. A lethal dose is said to be five hundred roentgens over the period of five hours, which means some workers received a deathly dose within a few minutes.

The initial fire was extinguished by 5am but the blaze deep inside the reactor continued burning until May 10th. The Chernobyl Power Station Firefighter Brigade's commander, Lieutenant Volodymyr Pravik, died on May 9th of acute radiation sickness, as did the reactor's senior engineer Leonid Toptunov. In the aftermath, two hundred and thirty seven people suffered from acute radiation sickness and more than thirty died within the first few months. Evacuees in the first ten days totalled one hundred and thirty five thousand, while six hundred thousand brave people risked their health to assist in the clean-up of the area over the next several years.

It was originally thought that the disaster was down to human error but a 1993 report from the IAEA Nuclear Safety Advisory Group, while acknowledging that human error did play a part, concluded that the two main reasons were the construction of the reactor and the peculiarity of physics. The RBMK type reactor, a Soviet model designed in the 1960s, was different from reactors in the west and didn't have the same safety features.

The reasons for what caused the disaster are, in a way, redundant now. While mistakes have to be examined to ensure they aren't repeated, analysing the situation won't improve the lives of those who have been left suffering in the disaster's wake.

Thirty seconds of chaos has led to twenty-five years and counting of misery, despair, poverty and illness. While the past can't be changed it can be remembered. And the greatest way to do this is by helping the present and future generations of Chernobyl's legacy.

This is the story of my own small attempt to do just that.

The Journey Begins

I was painting the frames and sills of our newly fitted windows when I first heard about the disaster. It's funny how the defining moments in life are recalled by such insignificant actions of the time.

The TV news played in the corner as I came indoors to wash the splashes of paint from my hands and the words accident, Chernobyl and explosion seemed to amplify over the sound of the running water. I quickly turned off the tap and went into the living room.

My hands drip-dried as I became engrossed in those early, sketchy reports after the Soviet regime had tried to suppress the disaster not just from the rest of the world but its own people.

The malignant monster had been unleashed. A number of people were dead or would soon die. Hundreds of thousands more were experiencing the end of life as they knew it.

Little did I realise that my life, too, would soon be forever changed by the world's worst nuclear accident.

In the years since I have often been asked why I feel so passionately about the explosion and fallout, why I have gone on to do what I do. My honest answer is, I don't know.

Perhaps it was my professional background that created my intense interest in the nuclear explosion. All my working life I was an electrician and in the late 1960s I worked in maintenance at the University of Glasgow. There were various radioactive sources on campus, including a large Particle Beam Accelerator in the basement of the Natural Philosophy building. Charged particles were accelerated through a gas chamber at incredible speeds and the results were captured on cameras for the scientists to examine the results. On several occasions we were working near the Synchrotron, as the apparatus was called, when the beam was due to be fired. Despite the huge, ten-ton door sealing the chamber entrance, we were iunstructed to evacuate the area.

That was just one of nearly two hundred jobs I had during my fifty year working life. I think the reason I moved around employers so often was I felt I should have been working at a much higher level than I ever managed to attain. The root of this feeling can probably be traced back to my childhood, a quite unpleasant period thanks to my school days.

I was born in the troubled times of World War Two, on January 8, 1941, into a working-class Glasgow family. I was brought up in a tenement on Willowbank Street, just off Woodlands Road in the West End of the city.

I didn't like school, especially primary, where my classmates and the teachers bullied me. I was naturally left-handed but the teachers would tie my left arm behind my back and force me to use my right hand. Anytime I tried to write with my left my knuckles would be struck with a wooden ruler and I spent many hours standing in the corner of the classroom wearing a dunce's hat. The school's brutal regime eventually enforced a permanent change and I have written with my right hand ever since.

Fortunately for my younger brother Peter, six years my junior and also left-handed, the school abandoned this humiliating practice by the time he started classes. I have since read that this draconian policy used by some schools could be extremely detrimental to a child's educational future. While Peter went onto be a successful businessman I was badly affected by the cruel procedure and left school at fourteen, so maybe there's something to that theory.

I spent a year at David Dale College in Glasgow, where it was possible to have a few weeks of training in various trades until deciding which one to learn full time. I decided on being an electrician and served my apprenticeship with various firms, starting with Glasgow Corporation. In those days it was commonplace to ask one of the numerous electrical firms in the city for work in the morning, leave your present job a few hours later and then start the new employment that same afternoon. I used to get fed up at times and needed a change, leading to many moves. I worked in Liverpool for three years and was also in the Territorial Army in Glasgow, followed by the RAF.

In 1968 though, I settled down when I married Margaret on March 29. We had two children - Jim in 1969 and Susan four years later. We moved to the "new town" of Cumbernauld in 1976, where Margaret and I have remained ever since. With a young family came holidays and before the days of employment rights I experienced the shocking but all-too-common practice of being sacked when requesting a holiday. Other bosses, meanwhile, would say it was all right to go on a break but then sack you on your return. This policy only added to the number of jobs I racked up.

I went back to work with Glasgow Corporation at their brand new state-of-the-art incinerator at Dawsholm in the early

1970s. I stuck it out for several years but eventually left because I just couldn't feel comfortable with the rats swarming everywhere – on the conveyors, in the electrical switch rooms, even amongst the waste paper. Over the years I've used my electrician skills on lifts, air conditioning, central heating, washing machines and general maintenance to name a few, most with more than one employer.

But through it all I was interested in nuclear power and that job at the University of Glasgow gave me the opportunity to ask the scientists about topics such as nuclear fission and the Windscale Fire in 1957. Windscale, now known as Sellafield, made weapons-grade plutonium, but on October 10 of that year Pile 1 overheated and the core went on fire. Radiation escaped from the reactor and into the air, before engineers brought the problem under control and put out the blaze before it led to catastrophe.

I have always viewed nuclear power as a potential threat to our safety, whether that is because of Windscale, seeing the powerful machinery firsthand in Glasgow University or the Three Mile Island meltdown in 1977 – or all three, I'm not sure. That perilous feeling prompted me to research and attempt to understand the workings and potential danger of nuclear power stations, so by the time of Chernobyl I already had a fundamental knowledge of its mechanisms.

As those tragic events slowly unfolded the truth emerged from behind the Iron Curtain of Soviet lies: tales of those brave firemen and soldiers fighting to extinguish the flames, of the mass evacuation of towns, of the hurt, the sacrifices and the deaths. I decided I wanted to find a way to remember the victims.

I watched the true extent of the horror become apparent and continually imagined what would happen should a similar nightmare on this scale happen in the UK. I thought of some of the nuclear stations relatively near my house in the West of Scotland – Sellafield in Cumbria, Hunterston in Ayrshire, Torness in Inverness and Dounreay in Caithness – and shuddered at what might be.

News emerged of the poor evacuees being shepherded onto buses, little realising they would never sleep in their homes again. Such a situation couldn't happen here, there are just too many people. Imagine trying to clear Glasgow should something awful happen at Hunterston. Impossible.

It was that human side of the disaster that really affected me and pulled at my insides. I just felt so sorry for these people. This was a catastrophic event that would haunt the world for a very long time and must be remembered. I felt I had to do something but what resources did I have at my disposal? Yet the media coverage showing the pain and suffering in explicit detail only strengthened my resolve.

It was then that I first thought of holding a vigil. For countless years all over the world vigils have been staged for many reasons; be it political, anti-war, civil rights and so much more. So I thought, Why not hold a vigil to remind people of the terrible event that occurred at 1.23am at the Chernobyl Nuclear Power Plant? It would be a dignified and peaceful way to keep the disaster, its immediate effects and its radioactive legacy for future generations, in people's minds. I was also aware it was something many in Ukraine might want to do themselves, but laws in the country at the time would prevent such an act.

Now that I had decided on staging a vigil, the planning could begin. But little did I realise the event would turn into an annual happening that became the foundation of my drive to help the Chernobyl victims.

The Vigils

I could never have imagined when I staged the first vigil in 1987 that I would still be marking the disaster three decades later, having never missed a year. But the most recent anniversary, on April 26, 2010, was also the one that came closest to passing by without the vigil.

Like thousands of people around the world, the ash cloud that swept across Europe following the eruption of the Eyjafjallajokull volcano in Iceland was placing my travel plans in serious doubt. Margaret and I were in South Africa visiting my brother, who had emigrated several years before. We were due to fly from Johannesburg late on April 22, but as that date neared it became apparent that we might not be going anywhere anytime soon. With Peter's internet connection down it made it even harder to keep updated with the latest travel situation and we were unable to speak on the telephone to anyone at KLM, our airline. So we visited the local KLM office, where we were told that our arranged flight to Amsterdam was still scheduled, but we had to sign a disclaimer stating we would be responsible for our own expenses should the connecting flight to Glasgow be cancelled if Scotland's airspace closed once again. The alternative was to stay in South Africa for another week and leave on May 3. Aware that I would miss the vigil if we did, we decided to take our chances and leave as scheduled.

Thankfully luck was on our side and we made it home to Cumbernauld without a glitch. Still recovering from the long flight, I made my way to George Square early on Monday the 26th, ready to begin my twenty-fourth vigil at 8am. By the end of the morning I would experience one of the most embarrassing and infuriating incidents from all the hundreds of hours of staging the event.

As I stood in front of my red stencilled sign, "Remember Chernobyl – Nuclear Power Disaster", a man came walking purposefully towards me. He was glaring at me and when he was close enough he yelled, "Take that banner down, I work for the council". He was spitting mad with anger.

I was rather taken aback by this. He had caught me unaware and I wasn't quite sure what his problem was; in my jacket pocket I had the letter of permission from Glasgow City Council, which I made certain to obtain every year. He continued walking as he stared at me and I was happy to see him stride off into the distance.

However, later in the day he returned. "I told you to take that sign down," he roared. "Take it down now, or I will." He was apoplectic. I looked around and saw a number of people in the bustling square staring at the two of us. He pointed at me with what appeared to be a metal walking pole he was carrying and turned to a nearby group of young people.

"This man's a tramp," he shouted towards them. "He's begging for money, don't give him any. Look at his pockets, they're bulging with the money he's collected."

I looked down at the pockets of my waterproof jacket. He

was right; they were bulging. Except one had sandwiches inside and the other contained a bottle of water. This man was really losing the plot now, big time. I had no idea if he was a council worker (as far as I could tell he wasn't wearing a council uniform) or a nut job, but I was mortified at his actions. I was also becoming quite angry.

But those feelings changed to fear when I saw him slipping his hand inside his anorak. My first thought was he was pulling a knife on me. I froze as I waited for him to pull his arm out. Instead he walked away, still glaring daggers at me. I, too, couldn't take my eyes off him as he marched to the edge of the road where, to my further amazement, he flagged down a passing police van.

"This is unbelievable", I muttered.

The so-called council worker began chatting with the officers inside the van and a few moments later a young policeman stepped out and came over to me.

"How are you?" he asked, smiling and shaking my hand.

I introduced myself and told him why I was there. I explained I had permission from the council to hold the vigil and produced the letter from my pocket. As he read it I told him I thought the person who had flagged his van down was a madman. I also said that I feared he might be carrying a knife. The policeman spoke to me for a few more minutes about my vigil before saying goodbye and returning to his van. From the angle the vehicle was parked I couldn't see whether that odious man was still there, but much to my relief I did not see him again for the rest of the day. I have no idea what his unsettling interruption was about, but I really hope Glasgow City Council does not employ such creatures to represent the city.

Those types of moments have been outweighed by the good, thankfully, but in 1987 as I planned the first vigil I had no idea what sort of reaction I would receive from the passing public.

The initial reaction from friends and family wasn't wholly positive. Margaret, my son Jim (eighteen at the time) and my fourteen-year-old daughter Susan, were concerned that I wouldn't be safe late at night, not to mention whether I would have enough to eat and drink. My parents thought the whole idea was a bit odd, while my friends wished me well. Over time they all grew used to it, and in later years it simply became known to family, friends, workmates and neighbours, as "Jim's Vigil Day".

Before I could stage the vigil I first had to decide where to hold it. George Square seemed the most obvious choice; it was in the centre of Glasgow and saw more people from all walks of life passing through it than most other places in the country.

I went to the City Chambers, which sits on the edge of the square, and asked for permission. I was told the area came under the provision of the Parks and Recreation Department around the corner in Trongate, so that was my next destination. I was given forms to fill in, which I returned a few days later, and was told a decision on my request would be made at the next scheduled departmental meeting. It was probably my naivety revealing itself, but I never imagined forms would have to completed and meetings would need to be held just to give me the go ahead to stand in George Square for a day.

Eventually I was granted permission subject to various rules and regulations - among them it stated I was responsible for crowd control and litter. No problem, I thought, it's just me and I'll put whatever rubbish I have in my pockets.

I knew I wanted some signs or posters to display but I couldn't afford to pay for placards to be made up and printed by a professional printer, so I decided to make my own. I bought an eight foot by four foot piece of hardboard with one side white and bought some stiff cardboard to make stencils. It took a long time to complete the alphabet and numbers stencil set, but once it was done I purchased a couple of permanent markers and began making my posters.

In the early years I displayed several placards, with slogans such as, "Britain Could Be Next" and "Privatised Nuclear Power Will Be Bad For Your Health". I usually stood next to a tree or streetlight where I could hang the posters. In later years I have taken just my original hardboard sign - which simply states, "Remember Chernobyl Nuclear Power Disaster", with that year's anniversary noted underneath - as it's easier to manoeuvre onto the bus.

The first vigil lasted twenty-four hours, but the experience persuaded me to cut the length in subsequent years. I started at eight am and in my mind divided the day into six four-hour blocks in the hope it would make it pass by a little easier. The first block was fine; as I arranged my posters quite a few people stopped to chat with me about what I was doing. "Has it been a year already?" and "I was working in my garden when I heard the news", were typical remarks from passers-by.

I had a small plastic bucket on the ground for donations and I'd collected a few pounds by the time an official from the Parks and Recreation Department came by and told me I wasn't permitted to receive donations from the public without a proper licence from the council. So that was that finished with.

The afternoon passed into evening and it was going well. People were stopping to talk about the disaster, so I felt I was doing what I had intended by keeping the incident fresh in people's minds. I had a small folding camp seat, so I sat down and ate some sandwiches I brought with me while I watched folk make their way home from work or pass through the square as they began a night out. When I needed to, I used the public toilets in nearby St Vincent Place, just a couple of minutes' walk away, but tried to drink very little to keep the breaks to a minimum.

From eight pm until midnight it was becoming a little more difficult due to the drinkers. Many of them were coming over to me and giving me hassle. Some were in squads and were quite intimidating. I pretended to ignore them in the hope they would go away, but I had to watch closely because they were aggressive. One guy staggered past shouting all sorts of abuse at me, but his equally drunk friends pulled him away and towards Queen Street station, presumably for their last train home. I pitied the railway staff that had to deal with them, but I was glad they were no longer in my vicinity.

From midnight until four am there were sporadic bursts of activity followed by lulls of quiet as revellers left clubs or moved from venue to venue. Some people were fine and passed without a problem, others shouted and swore in my direction. I was relieved when things quietened down.

The city seemed to take on a different atmosphere and feeling in those final four hours of the vigil. I was very tired by now, making this last block seem much longer than the rest, but I turned my thoughts to the plight of the families who had been evacuated from their homes and wondered how life was for them one year on. What would they be doing now, still under Soviet rule? Certainly no vigils for fear of arrest and imprisonment. I reminded myself I was doing something they were unable to do in Ukraine at that point.

This strange time of night that so few of us usually see unearthed a number of interesting characters whom I spoke with, including a man who told me he hadn't lived in a house for years and was quite happy to stay on the streets of various towns and cities. I couldn't imagine it; one day had been enough.

My experiences in the second half of the first vigil, when the sun set and the loons came out to play, made me re-evaluate my plans for future vigils. I decided they should last only twelve hours, from eight am until eight pm. That hasn't entirely cancelled out the threatening situations, although it's noticeably reduced the problem.

One of the nastiest incidents occurred towards the end of a vigil. While I leaned on an armrest of one of the square's wooden benches, four men in their late twenties strutted towards me. I braced myself for what I knew wasn't going to be a chat about the dangers of nuclear power.

"Give us yer fags and money," one of them demanded, flanked by the other three brutes.

Instinctively I stood up as they confronted me. "I don't smoke and I don't have any money on me," I replied.

"You lookin' for a fight?" another asked.

I just stared at him and didn't say a word. It was a fraught, worrying situation. A stand-off where there would be only one winner, and it wouldn't be me. I stood my ground and tried to appear calm and unflustered as the sweat rolled down my spine and my heart pounded.

Thankfully, after a few moments that felt like hours, they backed off and walked away, muttering obscenities towards me as they went. I knew I was lucky the situation hadn't escalated and I breathed a sigh of relief. I could also feel my blood boil because here I was, holding a vigil to remind people of a terrible event, and cretins like this come along. I was born and bred in Glasgow and its image has improved over the years, but turn over one of the many stones and see the creatures that lie beneath.

So far I have failed to paint a rosy picture of my vigils or my home city, but I have honestly had far more rewarding and worthwhile experiences than negative in the past twenty-five years. Countless people of all backgrounds have taken time out of their days to speak with me; students and businessmen, old ladies and drunks, crazies and Lord Provosts.

After a year or two of staging the vigils I began handing letters into the City Chambers for the attention of the Lord Provost, asking if he or she might come across the road and say hello if they had time. Some have been able to while others have not. Provosts such as Pat Lally, Liz Cameron and Bob Winters made the effort to come and wish me well, which was really pleasing. On another occasion the Deputy Lord Provost of Edinburgh, Steve Cardownie, came to see me. It was a very wet day and he presented me with an Edinburgh City Council umbrella, which I still use now.

During my 1989 vigil, a couple of waitresses from the Copthorne Hotel (now the Millennium Hotel), which sits on George Square, brought me over a dinner. That was a really kind and unexpected gesture. After thanking them I sat down on my camp chair, shielded myself from the lashing rain with my umbrella, and ate the meal. Another year, some girls from the City Chambers brought me leftover food from a council reception. Another nice and thoughtful act.

Infrequently I have talked to people originally from Ukraine, Belarus and Russia during my vigils. Only a few, but those who did stop spoke with sadness about their relatives and friends back home.

As well as through the vigils, I have tried to gain both an understanding and at the same time generate publicity for nuclear power and its dangers in a variety of ways. I have gone to Dounreay power plant and stood outside with a placard that stated it was wrong for Scotland to have a breeder reactor that could cause a nuclear explosion due to the configuration of the fuel assembly.

I also took a tour of Torness with other members of the public. I wore my jacket with the slogan, "nuclear power is bad for your health". Some of the passing workers said they agreed with that sentiment. As an aside, when I went down to the Houses of Parliament wearing that jacket I was told I would not be allowed inside until I removed it and was warned that if I put it on inside I would be arrested. True democracy in my own country.

I've also had many interesting conversations with John Large, a nuclear engineer specialising in safety at nuclear power stations in the UK. He has written many articles for organisations such as Greenpeace about possible accident scenarios at British power stations but his opinions have been ignored by the operators and the government. He runs his own nuclear consultancy company in London nowadays.

Walter Patterson, a Canadian-born nuclear physicist, is another expert who has taken the time to talk with me. He has written many books on the subject and in 1972 became Friends of the Earth's first energy campaigner. He said he agreed with most of what John Large had told me.

As the years went by, the media began to take notice of my vigils. One of my intentions had been to increase the Chernobyl disaster's profile in my own country, so I was happy to speak with the reporters. The local radio station, Clyde, has interviewed me twice, as have a couple of newspapers, primarily the Evening Times.

Something quite extraordinary and kind happened in the aftermath of one of the Evening Times' articles a number of years ago. On the day of the vigil it printed my picture and a report about my charity work for Chernobyl. Later in the afternoon a woman approached me. She was clutching the opened newspaper and asked, "Are you Jim?"

"I am that," I replied.

"Here's £300 for the children." She handed me an envelope and rushed away.

I was completely stunned.

When I realised she was quickly disappearing into the passing crowd I shouted after her, "I'll write you a thank you note. What's your name?"

"Jim and Nancy," she responded, still walking. "We don't need a letter."

So, Jim and Nancy, if you happen to read this all these years later: thank you from the bottom of my heart.

That wasn't the first time I experienced such unexpected and apparently spontaneous generosity. In the early years another nice woman stopped to show an interest in what I was doing. Every year since, this kind elderly lady has given me a donation and in return I send her reports about my Ukrainian visits. She lives with her husband in Glasgow and wishes to remain anonymous, but I thank her very much for her wonderful support over the years.

While the media reports and visits from the Lord Provosts helped raise both the vigil's profile and the Chernobyl people's plight, I longed for a famous face to lend their name so as to give the project a high-profile boost.

Almost from the beginning I tried to contact celebrities to ask if they would offer support or join me on the vigil for a short time. I also wrote to big businesses and football clubs such as Rangers and Celtic. I watched fundraising events on television and wished I could organise a charity event, albeit on a smaller scale, for the Chernobyl victims. I thought if I could attract the interest of an internationally known singer, for example, they might be willing to stage a concert to raise money.

It was tough procuring the contact addresses of celebrities' agents in the days before the internet, but I did manage to write to a number of stars, albeit without success. All I received were polite rejections. Known musical humanitarians Joan Baez and Mike Rutherford, of Mike and the Mechanics, took the time to respond. I had asked each if they would consider holding a charity concert to raise funds for Chernobyl, but I think they misunderstood me because they seemed to believe I was asking them to play at a concert I was organising, whereas I hoped they would take matters into their own hands.

Mike Rutherford wrote, " Dear James, Thank you for your letter concerning your intended charity concert. Unfortunately I will not be able to take part in it because my time is pretty much accounted for with recording and other charity events until the end of the year."

On behalf of Joan Baez, Mark Spector wrote, "I could only discuss her participation in a fundraising concert upon receipt of much more detailed information than your letter provides."

I also received replies from TV personalities such as Eamonn Homes and John Pilger, who said they would consider doing pieces on the anniversaries of the disaster.

A letter arrived at my home on behalf of the most famous living Scotsman, Sean Connery. Dated March 7, 1997 and postmarked Casa Malibu in Malaga, Spain, it stated, "I regret to inform you that Mr Connery is unable to attend your annual vigil on the 26th of April as he is scheduled to be filming in the United States. Thank you for your invitation."

Veteran Scottish singer and entertainer Alastair McDonald called me upon receipt of my letter and took the time to chat. He said he would have come along to the vigil and sung a couple of songs, but unfortunately he had a broken ankle and was immobile.

And Norman Wisdom, one of my favourite entertainers from yesteryear and also a dedicated charity worker, sent a nice response to my letter. He said, "I am sorry to tell you that on the above date I have an engagement on the island that naturally precludes me from being with you. I can appreciate the terrible situation and conditions out there as I did go to Chernobyl four years ago, travelling by convoy with lots of equipment to see the completion of The Norman Wisdom Hospice for Sick Children. I hope you have a successful meeting."

While my attempts to garner the support of a big name personality or local celebrity have so far been in vain, I continue to try. I hold out hope that one day such a person will help, as they will be able to raise far more funds for the Chernobyl children than I could ever achieve myself.

However, no matter what happens, I will continue to hold my vigil in George Square every April 26 for as long as I am physically capable, and remember the tragic scenes that emanated from that horrible day.

The Road to Paris is Paved with Good Intentions, Bad Driving and Criminal Wrongdoing

I watched the TV news as EuroDisney opened its gates in a blaze of publicity in Marne-la-Valee, a new town approximately twenty miles from the centre of Paris, on April 12, 1992 following a protracted and controversy-ridden construction period.

Here was a state-of-the-art children's theme park, a far cry from the infamous images I'd seen of the rusted, abandoned Ferris wheel in the radiation-poisoned town of Pripyat, and it struck me that it would be quite appropriate to cycle to this new kids' fun park to help the sick children of Chernobyl.

I had been attempting to organise a fundraising event for some time. While the vigils were primarily intended to raise Chernobyl's profile and make sure the disaster wasn't forgotten, I also wished to raise money to help the children affected by the tragedy. Donations would come in from well-wishers, such as the ladies I mentioned who I met on the vigils, while friends and family also contributed generously. But I wanted to do something more to raise funds. I had always been quite active, going on leisure runs and cycling to and from work. So I decided to put those exertions to good use and started running half marathons and sponsored fun runs.

I had something bigger in mind though, and I was constantly thinking of ways to raise money. I asked for permission to wing-walk at my local airport; to abseil down a high-rise block, from a bridge, even down Blackpool Tower, but all I received was a series of "no, can't help, ask elsewhere" responses.

So the cycle ride to EuroDisney seemed perfect and it would require no authorisation from anyone in power (although Margaret was less than enamoured when I told her of my intentions!).

The previous longest cycle I'd done was around 140 miles to Dundee and back, and that was a couple of years earlier. The weather was perfect on that trip, practically windless, but I knew I could be facing all types of conditions on the road to Paris – even though the cycle was planned for the first two weeks of August. Much of the route would be undertaken in the British summertime, after all.

A lot of practice would be required to improve my stamina and fitness in the build-up to the trip. But a number of incidents while training out on the roads were, unfortunately, a sign of events to come. On an early practice cycle I was returning to Cumbernauld from Callander. Approaching Doune, I could sense a car slowing down as it neared me from behind. Then, as the car pulled round me, the passenger rolled down his window and swore as he threw a liquid over me. I slammed on my brakes. I looked at the substance that was splashed all over my clothes and bare legs. It had given me a real fright. I had no idea what it was; it could have been acid or petrol for all I knew. Thankfully it turned out to be harmless, probably just water or a drink of some kind, but it gave me a real fright.

Another time, going up the Crow Road in Lennoxtown, I heard a car racing towards me from the rear. It narrowly missed my right elbow as it passed and some young guys were hanging out the opened windows shouting abuse and giving me the V sign. A few centimetres nearer and I would have been struck, but I doubt they would have stopped to make sure I hadn't been hurt.

Returning home from Fintry one night in torrential rain, waiting at a junction in Denny, a large car driving in my direction slowed as it came alongside me. The passenger door opened and the man inside began shouting, swearing and threatening me with violence. Much to my relief the car drove off without further incident, but again this senseless piece of road rage scared me.

Unfortunately, abuse of cyclists has continued to increase over the years. In my opinion road rage has become a serious problem in our society, one that doesn't look like improving anytime soon. My family was concerned about my safety when I told them about my planned EuroDisney trip, because they knew I would be travelling on a lot of unfamiliar roads with fast moving traffic. I omitted to tell them about the many dangerous run-ins I had experienced during the months of training, as it would only cause more worry. I had cycled a little on foreign roads before this trip - in Holland and Belgium while I was working in the Gorinchem shipyard in the Netherlands for five weeks in 1990 – but nothing extensive.

My planning continued. I studied maps of Britain and France

and highlighted my route, and then placed them in polythene pockets so they would remain dry should I have to check the directions while out in the elements. I took my cycle jacket to a print company and had "Cycling Scotland to Paris to help the children of Chernobyl" printed in red on the back, while on the front it read, "De Ecosse A Paris pour aider les enfants de Chernobyl", so the French people could also understand what I was trying to accomplish.

I contacted the media in the hope they would publicise my attempts, and in turn entice individuals or businesses to give donations. But disappointingly I received very little coverage, only a small piece on Radio Clyde's news bulletin and a mention on the Ukrainian broadcasting division of the BBC.

I pressed on with the final preparations as August approached. I was on the dole at the time so not having to arrange time off work meant one less thing to do. My aim was to cycle one hundred miles each day, which would equate to between eleven and fourteen hours in the saddle. I knew it was going to be difficult but I was determined.

It was the morning of August 1. My bike panniers were packed with clothes and I also filled a backpack with essential gear: a few sandwiches, water, fruit, energy bars, a puncture repair kit, spare chain, lamp batteries, gear change, brake cables and various tools. The local councillor had invited me to leave from the council offices, where there was a small send off from Margaret, her mum and my mum, my daughter Susan, and one or two other family members, friends and the councillor.

They cheered me off as I cycled along the level road of Bron Way, and then downhill towards Luggiebank. But my first challenge came as I climbed towards Airdrie Road. I could feel every ounce of weight in my panniers and backpack as I slowly struggled uphill, my legs feeling the early strain as I pushed down on the pedals and a dry, rough sensation forming in the back of my throat as I struggled for breathe.

Doubts crept into my mind. If I were feeling the heat already, how could I possibly manage fourteen hours on the saddle? Be positive, I told myself. I can do it. This is just the first step and hundreds of miles lie ahead. I reminded myself why I was doing it, which helped me break through that first barrier and find my stride.

I eased myself in gently that first day and only cycled around seventy miles, stopping for the night at Melrose Youth Hostel. I was a youth hostel member and I intended to stay in as many as I could to keep down the costs of the trip. The following morning I started early and made good progress. But the first scary incident of the trip happened as I came into Salford, Manchester.

I was at traffic lights at a busy crossroads, waiting to go straight across the junction. To my right was a long articulated truck also going straight ahead. At the far side of the junction on my left was a petrol station. As the traffic lights turned green I pedalled off, but quickly I heard the noise of the truck accelerating and looking over my shoulder I saw the rear wheels of the vehicle coming dangerously close towards me. I swerved into the filling station forecourt just as the tyres mounted the pavement edge. The truck never stopped. I don't think the driver had any idea I was there, far less how near he had come to wiping me off the road. He may have felt a slight jolt when he clipped the kerb, but that jolt could easily have been my bike and me. That scary incident prompted me to call it a day soon afterwards.

Monday morning brought with it rain. Before I set off on the next leg I decided to mail a postcard back home but I needed a stamp, so I stopped outside a newsagent as I passed through the Moss Side area of the city. I looked through the shop window and saw the counter at the far end of the empty shop. I would only be a few seconds.

I leaned my bike against the window and went inside. I turned and looked at the bike as I approached the shopkeeper, just to check it was ok. I reached under my cycle cape and waterproof trousers for money, and then looked back at my bike again.

Except this time my bike wasn't there.

It had only been seconds. Surely it must have just slipped down the glass onto the ground?

I rushed outside to look. I had an awful sinking feeling in my stomach when I saw it was gone. Not on the ground, not leaning against the wall, not being pedalled away by a brass-necked thief.

I ran back into the store and explained to the shopkeeper what had happened. He called the police. While I waited for them to come I looked around outside rather futilely, but there was no sign of my bike. When two officers arrived in a patrol car they explained that I was in a fairly bad area of the city, not that I could have known that as a stranger.

They offered to drive me around the streets in the hope we might spot the crook. We crept up and down narrow alleyways at the back of terraced houses, similar to the ones seen on Coronation Street's opening credits, while one of the officers explained that the area was rife with drug dealers who employed boys to act as couriers. Apparently the young lads would use stolen bikes to move between drop-offs, and it looked like today it was my mountain bike that had been used for illicit transportation.

The search was proving useless so they drove me to the local police station to make a statement. I was still shocked, not to mention angry, and the cup of tea they gave me did little to calm my nerves.

Once the officers had as much detail as I could provide I made my way out onto the unfamiliar, and suddenly quite daunting, Manchester streets. I almost felt like a drifter, wandering around lost and unsure how to get myself out of this predicament.

My head was muddled and I felt quite nauseous as I tried to digest the reality that was staring me in the face - that my trip to EuroDisney was over before I'd gone much more than two hundred miles from home. I was gutted. Absolutely sickened. If I had just chained the bike up, I found myself thinking, this wouldn't have happened. But the shop was empty and I was only going in for a stamp; it would have taken more time to attach the chain than it would to go in and out of the store. Now I wished I had taken those extra few seconds to secure my bike.

I walked around in a daze for who knows how long, trying to collect myself together and decide how I would return home. I had lost everything except the clothes on my back and the wallet in my pocket.

I looked up and saw the Piccadilly Hotel across the road. I could see there was a bar on the ground floor, so I decided to go in and have a cup of coffee and a scone while deciding what, if anything, I could do.

As I thoughtlessly swirled the spoon round and round in the mug, I looked up and saw a public phone at the bar. I should probably call Margaret and tell her what had happened, I decided.

"What can you do?" she asked, once I'd recounted the story.

"Not much," I muttered despondently. "Maybe it'll be found."
I was trying to be positive for Margaret's sake, but I didn't really
believe this statement to be true. "I'll phone you later," I added.
"But it looks like I'll be coming home tomorrow."

As I hung up the phone and turned to go back to my seat, a
stocky, middle-aged man approached me.

"I saw your jacket while you were on the phone. Are you really cycling from Scotland to France?" he asked.

I told him that had been my intention, but it seemed unlikely
now. I repeated the story I had just told Margaret and the police
before her; it didn't get any better with each retelling.

"That's terrible," he said. "Would you like a loan of a bike to
allow you to continue?"

Would I! My eyes lit up when I realised the cycle ride might
not be over after all.

"That would be tremendous," I exclaimed. "Thank you so
much." I shook his hand and realised I didn't even know the
name of this Good Samaritan.

"It's George Little. Now listen, this is what we'll do. Tonight
you will stay in this hotel, have your dinner, and in the morning
have breakfast. By the time you've eaten your breakfast a bike
will have been delivered here. It's just a basic model without any
fancy gears or add-ons, but hopefully it'll do the job for you.

"I'm a retired fire officer," he continued, reaching into his
pocket. He brought out what looked like a business card. "This
is my fire service social club card. If you show this at any fire station on your way down south and explain your circumstances
and what you're doing, you'll be given a bed for the night."

I couldn't believe the generosity this man was showing to a
stranger. It was quite overwhelming.

"Thank you so much, Mr Little. I'll gratefully take the bike but you can't possibly pay for me to stay here this evening. That's too much."

But he insisted. "I admire what you're doing to help children affected by Chernobyl and it's a pleasure not only to loan you a bike, but to pay for a night's accommodation, too."

I had gone from the doldrums to feeling sky high within a few moments. This was all too much. Mr Little may have been his name, but he was certainly big in heart and kindness.

He gave me a note of his address so I could return the bike on my way back from Paris, and then he booked a room for me at reception. I looked on, still in disbelief, and thanked him again and again. With that he was gone, just as quickly as he had appeared.

I called home again, this time to give Margaret much better news. She too was amazed by this stranger's generosity and she was happy for me, although she still noted a word of caution about my well-being for the rest of the trip. Not only was she still concerned about the dangers of the fast-moving traffic on the unfamiliar roads, now she also had the prospect of muggers, thieves and the like to make her ill at ease. However, I had to believe that what happened that morning was a one-off, and the generosity of George Little was the rule rather than the exception.

After a good night's sleep and a hearty breakfast I felt ready to plough on with the trek and put the previous day's setback beyond me. As George had promised a bike duly arrived, delivered in a small fire service van by two firemen who wished me all the best.

I was, literally, back in the saddle.

The bike was basic, as George had warned, and it had nothing close to the range of gears and extra features that my stolen bike was adorned with, but it had two wheels and that was the most important thing for now. Although it was a heavier bike, because I had nothing left to carry the effort to pedal was about the same as before.

The day's cycle passed without incident, thankfully. In the evening I located a fire station and presented George Little's card at reception. I explained what I was doing and, just like he said they would, I was welcomed in with open arms by the firefighters. They gave me a room to myself, more than I expected. A fireman explained to me that should the alarm ring all the lights would automatically come on. He added, jokingly, that I would not be required to respond. It was a quiet night; although I was so exhausted I would likely have slept through any number of interruptions. In the morning I was treated to a full breakfast and big mug of tea, and with their best wishes I set off once again.

It was Wednesday, August 5, the fifth day of the cycle. It had been much more eventful than I had expected, or wanted, so far. The rain had been pouring down earlier in the day, but as I journeyed along a dual carriageway towards Stafford, the conditions improved and the sun shone.

I moved across the road to make a right hand turn. I watched as a car drove slowly towards me from a side road. I expected he was turning to run parallel with me, but instead he drove straight out and banged against the side of my bike. I thumped to the ground, landing hard on my hip. Although the vehicle had been moving slowly I still took quite a dunt when hitting the road. I lay dazed and shaken and as I counted the stars I wondered what else was going to go wrong? I began to think the cycle was ill-fated.

The driver jumped out of the car and rushed over. He was most apologetic. "Sorry, I never saw you. Are you hurt? Do you need anything?"

He looked as stunned as I felt.

I was more concerned about the damage done to the bike rather than any injury I might have suffered. I felt fine apart from the shock and I could easily carry on with a few bruises, but if the bike was broken then the cycle was in peril once again. I struggled to my feet and picked up the bicycle. The handlebars were twisted loose, which I easily sorted, but apart from that it seemed unaffected by the crash. I was lucky.

Just then a police car happened to pass by. When the officers saw the accident they came over and checked on us and insisted on calling an ambulance for me. The driver and I gave statements while I waited for the paramedics. When they arrived they demanded I go to the local hospital. I was anxious just to be on my way, but they were adamant.

The car driver, who was actually a really nice fellow, followed me to casualty and waited while I was looked over. When we'd arrived at the hospital the ambulance crew told the doctors that I was on a charity cycle ride and requested that I be checked over as quickly as possible so I could be on my way again. The diagnosis was just a few cuts and bruises, meaning I was free to go. The doctors added that what I was doing was admirable and they hoped the rest of my trip was accident-free. So did I.

Before I left hospital, I thought I should call Margaret to tell her about my latest close call. I looked at my watch and realised she would still be at work, so instead I called Radio Clyde. I had been trying to drum up some publicity, so I thought this might get people's attention. What I failed to consider was that some of my family might hear the news bulletins and receive a shock.

The car driver insisted he take me on a shopping trip to buy some new clothes. He had seen my jacket with its message and I had told him about my so far cursed trip that had left me without even a change of clothes. He insisted he do something to help, so bought me a few casual shirts and underwear.

Eventually I returned to the road, shaken and a little sore, but just glad to be making progress after so many wasted hours. Each setback only made me more determined to complete the challenge.

I found a nice looking bed and breakfast to spend the night. After I explained what had happened in Manchester, the owners allowed me to park my bike to the rear of their home.

When I called Margaret her voice was frantic with worry. "Are you hurt?" she exclaimed.

I realised then my mistake in calling Radio Clyde. One of our neighbours had heard about the accident on the news and when Margaret came home from work she was asked by the neighbour if I was all right. Of course, Margaret had no idea what she was talking about. This wasn't the best way for her to find out, to put it mildly. She and the rest of the family were frantic with worry because all they knew was I had been knocked down. In these days before mobile phones they just had to wait for me to be in touch. Margaret was very relieved to hear I was OK, but it did little to quell her concerns about her husband cycling on busy roads.

The B&B had a number of guests and upon noticing my jacket they were intrigued to hear my story. When I went to pay my bill the following morning, the landlady told me one of the other guests had already settled it. I was left humbled by another person's kindness yet again.

Back on the road, I continued heading south until finally I arrived at Dover. On the ferry I washed some of my clothes and had something to eat. When we docked at Calais, I walked off the boat with only a loaned bike and a polythene bag containing the wet clothes, a razor, a bottle of water and a cheese sandwich.

As I pedalled from the ferry port into mainland France I felt I had achieved something just making it this far, all things considered.

Bearing in mind those calamities in England, the trip across France passed by serenely. I found my way without too much bother, despite the lack of maps. Had the constant danger from motorists passing too closely and quickly not still have been tantamount in my thoughts, then it would have proved quite a pleasant ride. Time and time again, stupid and ignorant drivers passed by at speed leaving just inches between their vehicles and myself. The abundant amount of roadkill I had to avoid was staggering. Foxes, rabbits, badgers, deer, dogs, cats – it was endless and morose. I was all too aware if I were struck it would likely result in a terminal outcome, just like the animals.

Seven long and punishing days after leaving Cumbernauld I arrived in Marne-la-Valee and at the bustling entrance to EuroDisney. My intention was always to go inside and have my picture snapped beside one of the famous rides or landmarks replicated from Disney's parks in America, but when I asked the officials at the front gates I was told that wouldn't be possible.

I explained the purpose of my trip and pointed to the words on my jacket, but they were adamant in their refusal. I asked if

I could speak with a manager but this, too, was not possible. A ticket attendant gave me ten free passes for the park, probably more as a gesture to move me on rather than for any benevolent reason. Later I thought I might be able to raffle these off to raise money for Chernobyl victims, but without flights and accommodation it wasn't much of a prize. The passes are probably still at the back of a drawer in my home to this day.

With the officials resolute in their stance, I asked a member of the public if he would mind taking a picture of me in front of the golden entrance gates.

With that done I immediately began my journey back to Scotland. I was bitterly disappointed and disillusioned in the attitude of the EuroDisney staff. All I wanted to do now was go home, so much so that I didn't even stop to look at the famous Paris sights.

The return cycle was mercifully uneventful but quite tough mentally and physically. On the first leg there was a purpose and aim, but now that I had made it to EuroDisney and received such a tepid and disenchanting reaction, the road seemed twice as long and doubly hard.

Only one happening on the journey back is worth noting, and this time it was me falling foul of the law.

I was cycling towards the Blackwall Tunnel, road tunnels underneath the River Thames in London, when I paused to have a drink of water and an apple. I lifted my bike off the road and over a crash barrier, and rested on the handlebars while I took a break. Just then a police car pulled up beside me and asked where I thought I was going. Apparently cyclists were not allowed on this stretch of road or through the tunnel. I had no idea and didn't see any signs stating no entry to bicycles, but

I suppose there must have been. One of the officers told me I would not be charged on this occasion, but I would have to make my way off at the next slip road. Quite embarrassingly, the police car followed me at close juncture with its blue flashing lights alerting other road users to my faux pas.

From there it was destination Manchester, to return the bike. Once I found his house, Mr Little answered the door and I thanked him once again for the loan. He said few words in response, which seemed quite strange considering all he had done for me and the interest he had shown ten or eleven days earlier. I left the bike by the front door where he kept me standing and thanked him again, before walking into the city centre to hopefully catch a bus back to Scotland.

I only had a few hours to wait. A bus departed for Glasgow at 6pm and I returned home to Cumbernauld in the early hours, never more thankful to be back in my own house and to see Margaret. It had been a long and eventful two weeks and I couldn't help but ask myself if it had been worth it.

When the final amount of donations and sponsorships came in I realised I'd raised only £100, mainly thanks to family and friends. I had hoped to raise funds and bolster the profile of the children in Ukraine, but neither had happened. It actually cost more money to go than I had managed to raise. I put the £100 into my fund and vowed to continue thinking of ways that would help the Chernobyl kids.

I wasn't ready to call it quits, not by a long shot.

The bad experiences on the road to Paris weren't enough to put me off cycling. I still ventured out on my bike regularly and, as the years passed and I became a frequent traveller to Ukraine, I had another idea for a sponsored cycle ride. This time, I thought, why not cycle all the way from my home in Cumbernauld to Kiev?

I'd been contemplating the two thousand mile ride for a long time. Now, in the second half of 2005 and just months before my sixty-fifth birthday, I decided to go for it.

Margaret wasn't happy with the idea. She said it was too dangerous and she was right; it would be perilous. Apart from the usual dangers that cyclists face on the road, I knew passing through sections of Poland wouldn't be safe and the number of bandits in Ukraine might also prove hazardous. But I couldn't think that way; the focus had to be firmly on the ultimate aim and the rewards that accompanied it, because surely such a journey would raise lots of funds.

I knew I wasn't as young as when I took on the Paris ride. More than a decade had passed. But I was fit and had been going out on the bike often to prepare for my planned one hundred mile daily trek through England, France, Belgium, Germany, Poland and finally Ukraine.

Throughout the summer of 2005 I increased the distance I cycled each night to build up my stamina and strength for the real thing.

The sunny Sunday afternoon of July 9th was one such occasion. I had cycled to Stirling and was on my way back home (approximately a forty mile round trip) when a terrifying incident abruptly ended my cross continent cycle plans.

I was passing through Denny, a small town a short distance from Falkirk, in perfect conditions. The sunshine reflected on my yellow high visibility jacket as I went by the local high school. From here I stopped at a tee junction, turned right and cycled up a hill. As I reached the crescent, there was another tee junction to my left. A new-looking car driven by a solo female driver was at the junction, waiting for me to pass in order to make a right turn across my path.

Or so I thought.

I was cycling by her, in line with the car bonnet, when suddenly she pulled out.

"Stop!" I yelled. "Stop the car!"

But the car continued to move.

I thudded against the vehicle, striking my spine. The car was beside me, and my strewn body was positioned between her offside wing and the bonnet.

All sorts of thoughts raced through my head when I realised she was continuing her manoeuvre. As the car moved round the corner, my twisted body was thumped, banged and dragged. I was flipped against the driver's door, which I slid down and fell onto the ground.

"Stop! Please stop the car!" I was screaming, but still the driver carried on.

As I lay prone on the road I had the wherewithal to notice the rear wheel of the car was coming towards my head. I was going to die if I didn't move.

With my trembling left hand I managed to push my head away from the tyre. Just as I did so I felt an incredibly painful pressure on my left elbow.

I screamed in agony. She had run over my arm.

Finally the car stopped. By now I lay crumpled and stricken in the middle of the quiet road. The shock kicked in and I don't remember much after that.

I can recall the young lady, aged around thirty years old, repeatedly saying she didn't see me. She said the same thing when the police and ambulance arrived. I was wearing a high visibility jacket, it was a bright afternoon and it was a clear stretch of road. Despite all that she couldn't see me approaching. It seemed her hearing wasn't too good either, because I had screamed and yelled and been thrown against her car.

When I was taken into the ambulance I called Margaret from my mobile and told her I had a puncture and would be delayed. I didn't want her to worry. I also knew it would only strengthen her feelings against me undertaking the bike ride to Ukraine.

I was checked over at the accident and emergency ward at the Royal Infirmary in Stirling. Some time had passed, so I thought it best to call Margaret again to let her know I would be further delayed.

"Margaret, my chain is broken as well. I'm going to be a while longer."

"Are you in the hospital?" she replied, her voice fraught with worry.

"What do you mean?" I stammered.

How did she know? In retrospect it must have been quite obvious that something was wrong but at the time in my cloudy head I didn't realise.

My daughter Susan drove Margaret to the hospital to pick me up. Luckily I suffered no broken limbs, although the bone in my left elbow was damaged and still aches at times. Considering what would have happened had I not moved my head from the oncoming wheel, I was very fortunate indeed.

Margaret was worried sick. She was also angry, and while Susan drove us back to Cumbernauld my wife made it clear there was no way I was cycling to Ukraine after this accident.

If this could happen so close to home, what might happen on foreign roads in Europe?

So to the relief of my family I grudgingly cancelled the trip.

I still harbour hopes of one day embarking on a long distance bike ride but I don't know if it will ever come to pass. The accident hasn't put me off cycling completely; I've been doing it too long to give up.

But whether I will ever cycle for anything other than pleasure again, I can't say with any certainty.

Everything Changes

I studied the envelope the postman had just dropped through the door, unaware that the letter inside would eventually change my life. I was intrigued by the handwriting, loose and somewhat awkward, which erroneously noted my address, although it was close enough to reach my letterbox.

Opening the envelope I pulled out a folded sheet of paper and sat down at the kitchen table to read the short and mysterious note, also handwritten.

"Dear Mr James Gillies!" the letter began. "I will be glad to meet you as I will help the victims of Chernobyl too."

What is this about, I thought. Who is this from? I looked to the bottom of the letter. There was no name. I continued reading.

"I'm a student. I study English and German in Kiev. My parents live in a village situated at a distance of 70 kilometres from Chernobyl. The ecological situation is very hard. I suggest to you a concrete business: you will write to me (to tell me) when you can come and we decide what to do. We can do together very much. If you want to do a concrete business, if you want to help the Chernobyl's victims, write to - "

There was a four line address that appeared to be written in Russian or Ukraine. And that was it. The end.

I looked at the envelope again in the hope that the sender's name was written somewhere. Nothing there but the unusual stamps. I flipped over the sheet of paper and looked at the reverse side. Completely blank.

I read the letter again. And again. It made no sense. I understood what this person was asking but what I couldn't grasp was how he had come to know who I was, where I lived or that I had an interest in Chernobyl and in trying to help its victims.

I had no connections or friends in Ukraine, as much as I wished I had, and no associations with any organisations based in the country.

This was a complete mystery.

I showed the letter to Margaret, to my kids and to other family and friends. They were equally nonplussed.

There was nothing else for it. I had to write back to find out who he was and exactly what he wanted. It never crossed my mind that the letter writer might not be genuine or that he could be playing a prank. Perhaps that was a little naive of me, but that's just how I am.

So I wrote a short letter stating my interest in Chernobyl and expressing my desire to help the victims. I mentioned briefly the vigils I held each year, although I wasn't sure if this might already be known to him. I asked him how he felt I could help? Why did he want me to go over to Kiev and meet him? What was his name? I tried my best to replicate on the envelope the address he'd provided, hoping it was clear and accurate enough to reach him.

Many weeks passed, perhaps months, and I began to doubt whether the letter had found its destination. But just when I was giving up hope, another letter bearing familiar handwriting and Ukrainian postage markings arrived on my doorstep.

"Dear Mr James Gillies!

"My name is Alexandr (Sasha), my surname is Lavrinenko. I'm very thankful for your letter to me, for your worry about the Chernobyl victims.

"I would like to write that my sister is working as a medical nurse in the district polyclinic. She works in the children's department. I think we can get information about the children's health in Malin district (it is my district where my parents are living). My village is Pirozhki. It is not a very large village.

"I think you can get government permission to do charity. But I know only your name and your surname. Write to me, please. Who are you? What is your profession? Strictly speaking the more information I can apply to the Ukraine government. (sic)

"I believe that we can visit Pripiyat, Chernobyl, Nazodichi. I'm living 70 miles from Chernobyl. I think that is not very long distance for the radiation.

"We are eating all provisions now. We grow potatoes, cucumbers, tomatoes and all the rest. Nobody pays attention to the radiation. What can we do? All people must eat. It is a law of the life.

"I will send to you a scheme of the radioactive contamination of the Zesium 137 in my Malin district. My district was in luck with the radiation. The level of radiation is below as in all other districts.

"I'm waiting for your letter. Yours sincerely, Alexandr."

I stared at the letter, trying to digest it all. This was the first time I had heard of Malin or the town's hospital. Little did I know just how familiar I would eventually become with both. Looking back now, this was a pivotal, defining moment in my life.

I was surprised to see him mentioning the Ukrainian government. I didn't know anything about the workings of his country at this time. Therefore maybe I wasn't best placed to go to the Ukrainian rulers and ask for money to help the children.

And what of those kids? I had seen enough news reports and documentaries to know they were likely to be very ill, maybe even suffering from horrific deformities and life-threatening cancers. I would do anything possible to help the children where Alexandr's sister worked. But that was the problem; what could I do on the opposite side of the continent?

It was also disturbing to read that Alexandr's home village was just seventy miles from Chernobyl, yet he felt they had got off lightly and were now eating the food crops. Who knows what harm they were doing their bodies by consuming the produce from contaminated soil and trees. But as Alexandr said, the people had to eat something.

I wrote Alexandr another letter in response, raising my questions and offering more information about myself. I asked if he had a telephone number that I could call him on, as the exchange of letters was proving very slow. I also stated how much I would like to help the children at the hospital, but wasn't sure how.

Again, a long time passed before I received another letter. When it did arrive it was even more shocking and eye-opening. A very specific request was made of me that I wasn't sure I was in a position to acquiesce.

"Dear James, I'm very thankful about your cares about the children which are living in the contaminated zone. The life here is very heavy. The people are working and eating the contaminated foodstuffs.

"My mother stands up at 5 o'clock every morning and goes to the farm. She goes here three times every day and gets approximately 200 roubles every month. In our shops we can buy not very much.

"This year the weather was very bad. At first it was raining and after that very hot (30-40 degrees above zero). And now we have no apples (I don't speak about the rest of fruits).

"It will be very well if you can send fruits and juices. I can promise you that the help will get to the children. But it must only be the private initiative. Before, the West was sending the help for the Chernobyl victims. My sister said that only one time they received it.

"I was in the clinic yesterday. I visited my sister and spoke with her and the head of the children's department. They were very surprised and did not believe me. I said to them that it was the truth. That one man from Scotland wanted to help. They gave me this list. These things are very necessary for them. If you need some more documents write to me. I can send to you or come to you.

"I have not a telephone. I have not a flat. In Kiev it is possible to buy a flat but it needs currency. I would like to come to the West and get money. It is not very much (9000 dollars) for the West people but for the Soviet people it is very much.

"My sister said that some children were ill with leukaemia in one region. They are now in Kiev. If you can (indeterminable word) for the treatment it would be very well. Write to me if it is possible. Please write your telephone number. I think that in some weeks or months will be found one or more children with this diagnosis.

"And now I would like to write the translation of this official list. If it is not very correct, I'm sorry for my mistaken (sic).

"Malin central region clinic. 1. The surgical sterile material. 2. The catheter for catheterisation of the vessels. 3. The one time systems for the transfusion of the blood and of the blood substitutes. 4. The collections of the surgical instruments – a) ophthalmologic b) otorhinolaryngologic c) general surgical. 5. The children's nourishment. 6. Fruits and juices, oranges, mandarins and apples.

"That is all. I'm sorry for my grammar mistaken. I'm waiting for your letter. Sincerely Alexandr."

I could not begin to imagine how bad the situation must be that the head doctors in a children's hospital ward would write a list of urgent supplies, requested by a nurse's student brother, to give to a faceless foreigner thousands of miles away. They surely couldn't have believed a stranger from Scotland would really be willing to help, yet they compiled a list. It was probably more out of desperation and abject hope than of real belief. That said it all.

But I really was willing to help. I just didn't know how to go about it. I wrote to Alexandr and told him exactly that. I didn't have the means at my disposal to gather the medical supplies he quoted, neither did I know how to deliver them even if I had.

It was distressing to read that two of the items on the doctors' list were simply "children's nourishment" and "fruits". It was almost incomprehensible to think that a hospital could not provide its young patients with basic food and vitamin intake. I had seen and read plenty of the suffering and poverty of the residents in the Chernobyl Zone, but hearing it personally from a first-hand source made it all more real, immediate and affecting.

I hoped Alexandr would be able to call me from a payphone or from his university so that we could discuss the many issues in more detail. But the call never came. Neither did the letter.

Months passed by in silence and I feared my Ukrainian link had been lost. I wrote to Alexandr again but still no reply. So instead I attempted to contact the hospital a couple of times. I never received a response but that wasn't a surprise considering I wasn't sure of the address and I was writing in English.

It was doubly frustrating because the mystery of how Alexandr had come to know of me and where I lived remained a mystery. He never explained in his letters how he had heard of Jim Gillies and my interest in the Chernobyl victims.

Incidentally, more than a decade later, I thought I was finally going to learn how Alexandr knew me when I met him in Ukraine. Scottish Television had accompanied me on this trip and they felt it would be interesting to meet the man who had set me on my path.

Via the hospital's staff records, Alexandr's sister (who had long since left her job) was tracked down and she in turn contacted him. I was really looking forward to meeting him and discovering the answer after all those years. But he had forgotten all of his English by the time we met and, even more disappointingly, he said he couldn't remember how he first heard of me. I couldn't believe it! All those years of wondering and I finally meet Alexandr face-to-face , only for him to have forgotten.

Going back to the months after the letters stopped, I didn't know what else to do. I hated the thought of the doctors forlornly waiting for supplies and the helpless children in Malin's hospital lying in their beds without so much as an orange. But I felt my hands were tied.

I wanted to try to help some of the victims, even if it couldn't be those in Malin hospital. I had heard of an organisation based in Doncaster called Golden Wheels, which was taking an aid convoy containing clothing and donated medicines from a hospital in Leeds, over to the Chernobyl area. It was organised by two gentlemen called Stephen Lelew and Steve Bomok, who I contacted and later met. They seemed like ideal conduits to deliver my help to the victims and so I handed over £240 to the charitable organisation when they visited Edinburgh on business.

In 1993 I watched a World In Action documentary about a remarkable woman called Nina Rogerson (maiden name Bogdanova). She was originally from Ukraine but moved to Britain in 1967 after she married an Englishman, and she now lived in Bolton. Her hometown is Chernigov, a town just forty miles from Chernobyl and badly affected by the radiation fallout. The TV programme showed her trying to relieve the suffering of disabled children in Chernigov and her dream of opening a specialised medical centre for the sick kids in the town. She began her efforts immediately after the disaster in 1986 and set up The Forgotten Children of Chernigov Charitable Trust.

I contacted the World In Action production team and they promised to pass my details onto her. A few weeks later she phoned me and we arranged to meet the next time she and her husband, Norman, were coming up to Scotland to visit a friend who lived in Ayr. She is a very nice person and cares so much about the suffering caused by Chernobyl. I was pleased to hand over £700 from my account, which I had raised by running a series of half marathons, to Nina's project. The following summer, 1995, I gave her a further £136.

When I explained to her that I had been looking for a route into Ukraine to help Chernobyl victims, especially the children, she said I could be one of her Scottish helpers along with her Ayrshire friend. However, at this time I felt unable to do anything more than donate the money, as I had no links with Ukraine that would offer any assistance in her efforts. When I watch Nina's World In Action documentary today, it reminds me just how little I knew about Ukraine or its mechanics in those days.

Nina, I'm glad to write, realised her ambition and opened a specialist centre in Chernigov. A French company who owned a building in the town handed it over to her and she, along with a group of doctors, created the Centre of Medical and Social Rehabilitation of Disabled Children. With the help of humanitarians and philanthropists from the UK, Belgium, Netherlands and America, as well as Ukrainian organisations and businesses, it officially opened on June 19, 1996.

It's the only establishment in the region for medical, psychological, pedagogical and social rehab of disabled children and children with health problems. Kids have two or three courses of twenty-eight days' treatment in the centre each year, and it is estimated that her efforts have helped over nine thousand children. The centre is still going strong today, although Nina announced in 2001 that she was taking a back seat after the birth of her second grandchild.

I was doing what I could to help the victims by donating money through various established organisations, but the letters from Alexandr still played on my mind and I really wished I could find a way to aid the kids of Malin hospital.

I thought if I could speak the language that might open some doors for me. There was nowhere to learn Ukrainian at the time, so I booked Russian evening classes in Strathclyde University at £115 per year. Unfortunately I struggled with every aspect, although I did enjoy interacting with the other students and the lecturers, Valya and Natasha. It upset me at the end of each year, having paid all that money, to fail the exams. In recent years the ILA, a Scottish Government scheme, gives a £200 allowance towards a university or college course to people who earn lower wages and I've taken advantage of this. I also used to attend free classes in the Pearce Institute in Govan, where people from former Soviet countries would meet. I was able to have tuition there but when they could no longer afford the room hire the class had to close. I've tried numerous "How to Learn Russian" books and videos, but they never worked. So while I can understand some Russian words and will attempt short sentences and questions, I don't have an efficient grasp on the language that allows me to communicate without a translator.

However, my situation was soon to change.

It all started with a small advert I spotted tucked away in the back pages of a magazine in 1998. A Ukrainian journalist called Anatoli Artemenko, who was working at the City University in London, was to deliver a lecture at the institute on the "Radiological Effects of Chernobyl". It sounded interesting, especially since it was to be delivered by someone who came from the country. I also thought there would be potential to meet people who might be able to help with the Malin situation.

I reserved a ticket and made my way down to London on the overnight bus. Once I was in the capital I located the university and took a seat outside the lecture room to have a rest. I was tired but looking forward to hearing about the disaster and its effects from someone who had firsthand experience of Chernobyl.

The lecture was as interesting as I'd hoped and afterwards I approached Anatoli while he talked to a group of fellow Ukrainian nationals. They were his friends and business associates, such as Lesija, who represented the Ukrainian Women's Association in Great Britain. I introduced myself and explained my interest in the Chernobyl victims. We sat down and began chatting, and I showed Anatoli the letters from Alexandr. I told him how much I wished to visit Malin and try to help the hospital, but had so far found it impossible to do so.

Anatoli was extremely congenial and, although he wasn't familiar with Malin or its hospital, he promised to find out exactly where it was. He was due to return to Ukraine the following year to continue his journalism career and with that in mind, he said that should I wish to visit Malin I would be welcome to stay with him and his wife, Elena, at their home in Kiev.

I couldn't believe it. This man had only just met me yet he was willing to help not only locate the hospital, but extend an invitation to stay with him. We exchanged telephone numbers and I thanked him profusely, but I had to rush away to catch the overnight bus back to Glasgow, because I had to work the next morning.

When the bus pulled into Buchanan Bus Station I was physically exhausted but mentally exhilarated by the previous night's events. I was so glad I'd decided to make the trip. Now, at long last, I had the opportunity to visit Ukraine and most importantly, Malin hospital. I went to work straight from the bus station tired but deliriously happy.

My immediate impressions of Anatoli from that first meeting were that he was a very intelligent, likeable man who would be willing to help me in any way he could. He told me had worked with Yorkshire TV, the BBC and other broadcasters during his stay in the UK, acting as an advisor and translator. He was multi-lingual; he spoke Ukrainian, Russian, English, Polish and German. Over the next months, before he moved from London, I called Anatoli on a number of occasions while he gathered information to help make my dream trip to Malin a reality.

By the time he moved back to Kiev, where he was a political journalist working for publications such as the Kiev Post and the entertainment and lifestyle magazine What's On, he had set the wheels in motion for my visit. He'd checked Malin's location and discovered it was around seventy-five miles from Kiev and fifty miles from Chernobyl, meaning it was in Zone Four of the affected region. Anatoli told me if I wished to go over I would need a visa, a letter of invitation from the hospital and a letter from him stating I would stay with him during my visit. It was probably my naivety again, but I never considered there would be so much paperwork and legislation required before I could enter the country.

It was quite a learning curve to obtain a visa, as I had never before applied for one. I made a number of calls to the Ukrainian Embassy in London to inquire about how to proceed but found it quite difficult to understand their heavily-accented, fast-paced English. Eventually I worked out that the visa section was only open for two hours per day, between 10am and noon. The number was always busy and it took several days and numerous attempts before I could speak to someone. When I did, a Ukrainian visa application form was sent to me to complete, which I had to return along with my passport, the £40 fee, and letters of invitation from the hospital and my host.

Anatoli contacted the hospital and arranged for them to write a letter. I don't know what the doctors must have thought of this request or of my intentions. Maybe they remembered the rumours of a stranger coming to help several years earlier. They might have written the invite without ever believing I would really show up. That was perfectly understandable. I wasn't sure I truly believed it was finally happening, either.

There were a number of questions I had to complete on the visa application form. I had to state which cities I would be visiting, my means of financial support, my place of entry into the country, my transportation details, and the purpose of the trip. That last one was easy – to go to the hospital and help the children.

The process was rather daunting. It gave me an idea of how Ukrainian and Russian citizens must have felt applying for permission to travel outside their countries. Over the years I've discovered that many of these people were virtual prisoners within their borders. Even today, this is often still the case.

This somewhat difficult and costly procedure I had to go through improved after a couple of years when a Ukrainian Embassy opened in Edinburgh, which meant I could make the hour's drive through there from my home and not have to pay for registered mail. The situation was made simpler again in 2003 when, upon my arrival at the Embassy, I was informed I no longer required a visa to enter Ukraine. The reason? The country was hosting the Eurovision Song Contest! Thankfully, this has remained in place ever since, making it much easier to arrange travel.

But back to the first trip and, having received the letters, (which made no mention of the date I might be arriving or the length of my stay) I posted them to London along with the application form. Meanwhile, I had to find a way to actually reach the country.

Firstly I looked at flying but it was too expensive. So then I investigated going by rail, but the possible routes involved a number of changes that would increase the time of travel as well as the costs. Eventually I decided the best method would be to take an overnight bus from Glasgow to London, and then wait around in the capital until late afternoon when I could catch a bus to Warsaw with the Eurolines travel company. I had ascertained there were trains from Warsaw to Kiev, although I was unable to find out how often these were or where exactly in the Polish city they departed. But I presumed I would be able to find out when I reached Warsaw.

The only other matter to take care of was arranging time off work. This was fairly easy, since I was working for an agency at that point. No holidays were paid, so time off was like being back on the dole. I took fourteen days off, almost half of which would be spent travelling.

My passport and visa arrived in the registered envelope I had paid extra for, time off work was arranged, and transport as far as Warsaw was booked. I was as ready as I would ever be.

The wish I'd harboured since 1988 was on the verge of being realised. In March 1999 I made my way into Glasgow with a packed rucksack over my shoulder and in my hand an empty notebook ready to be filled. My big adventure was about to begin and a new chapter in my life would soon be written. The next two weeks were to affect me greatly and provide me with a new outlook and a reinforced sense of purpose.

Everything was about to change.

A Long Journey into the Great Unkown

In the run-up to my first visit to Ukraine, Margaret expressed her concerns for my welfare. Apart from the fact I would be travelling alone on an overnight bus to London, followed by a day hanging around the Big Smoke waiting for the evening bus to Warsaw (a journey that would take two days), I still had no idea where and when the train to Kiev left the Polish city.

I was going to miss our wedding anniversary while I was away, a fact I hadn't even noticed until Margaret brought it to my attention. I had been so engrossed in trying to sort out my trip and ensuring that the visa and bus tickets were in order that it hadn't even crossed my mind.

I told her I would play the train arrangements from Poland by ear, a foreign concept to Margaret since she is a very organised woman. In retrospect, she's probably justified in her fears because over the years there is usually some kind of happening in my travels that validates her worries, as you will later read. However, for better or worse my travelling motto has always been: better to travel with an open hand than a closed fist.

With that philosophy in mind I made my way to

Buchanan Bus Station buzzing with excitement and nervous anticipation. I had bid farewell to Margaret and the family back in Cumbernauld. Although happy I was finally realising a long-held ambition, they couldn't help but continue to voice their fears right up until I left. I told them I would contact them in London, and then as soon as I was able once I reached Kiev.

Since I wasn't sure when that would be, because I had no idea if the Warsaw to Kiev train was daily or the exact time it would take, I omitted telling Anatoli I was travelling to Ukraine. He knew I was coming sometime soon but he didn't know exactly when. Neither his letter of invitation nor the hospital's letter was date specified. The visa gave me a window, too. I thought it would be a nice surprise if I turned up in Kiev and called Anatoli with the news once I was there. Looking back, maybe this wasn't the best idea. But it's what I did and it certainly added to the drama of the occasion.

I was embarking on an adventure. Boarding a bus in Glasgow may not seem like an adventure, of course, but I was thinking ahead to Victoria Bus Station in London. I had been there several times before but this time when I arrived, instead of heading out into the hustle and bustle of the city, I went to the international ticket office to check my baggage. It seemed quite odd showing my passport for a bus journey.

Later in the day, when I saw the bus with the destination board "Warsaw", my heart fluttered knowing the next part of my journey was about to begin. I walked forward with my fellow passengers, most of whom I soon realised were Poles returning home. The driver weighed my two bags and both were under the maximum weight of twenty kilos. One contained my documents, shaving kit, food, water and Russian language book, while the other had my clothes, some books about Scotland I planned to gift to people, and a few other odds and ends.

I took my seat on the bus and as we prepared to drive down to the channel ferry ports I couldn't quite believe I was on my way to Eastern Europe. So many years reading about Chernobyl, watching documentaries, holding vigils for these nameless but not faceless strangers that I somehow felt so close to and sympathised with, staging various sponsored events to raise money for the victims, receiving those mysterious letters from Alexandr Lavrinenko that I still read so often; as the bus drove to Dover, images from the past thirteen years rushed through my head like a familiar movie on fast forward.

The baggage and passport checks as I boarded the ferry to Calais were thorough, possibly because my final destination was a non-EU country. Once over the channel and back on land it was a new experience for me, because I had never travelled across Europe by bus before. We drove through France, Belgium and Germany to the Polish border control, where our documents were checked. I was wary about this but it passed without incident and we carried on after a short stop.

As the bus made its way through city after city I thought back to the time twenty years earlier when Margaret and I could have been visiting the Soviet Union, and maybe even the newly opened Chernobyl Nuclear Power Plant. I was working at the famous Yarrow shipbuilding site by the Clyde in 1979 when a letter was pinned up on the noticeboard from the STUC (Scottish Trade Union Congress). Their counterparts in the Soviet Union trade union had offered the chance for some Scots to fly over to their country to experience the working and social lives of its people.

There were two places up for grabs and those who purchased a lottery ticket at 25p were entered into a prize draw for the spots on the plane, which was due to depart Glasgow on July 15th for two weeks. The itinerary allowed for sightseeing in cities such as Moscow and Leningrad, as well as visits to industrial enterprises and social clubs where there would be a chance to speak with workers to discuss their jobs, social and cultural life. The aim of the entire trip was to broaden horizons and increase understanding between Scottish union members and the Soviet Union's counterparts.

I was lucky enough to win the draw and looked forward to going over with Margaret, but I hadn't thought it through and with it being in the middle of the summer holidays and with two young children, there was no way we could go on holiday for a fortnight and leave the kids, so I had to pass the tickets onto a workmate. With the first two reactors at Chernobyl opening in 1977 and 1978, it's not out with the realms of possibility that I might have been asked to visit some employees at their brand new nuclear power plant workplace and in the custom-built city where they lived, Pripyat.

A few kilometres into Polish territory the bus pulled into an old and weathered roadside restaurant. It was possible to change currency into Polish Zlotys here, which I did in order to buy a cheap bowl of soup and some bread. It was a challenge to ask for the items but eventually I made myself understood and I sat down at a Formica table decorated with a faded pattern, happy to be off the bus for a while. The coach journey was a test of endurance in a way, not to mention having to offset the frustration of boredom. But everything was a first-time experience and there were new and unusual sights and encounters all around,

so these weren't big issues. I was like a kid in a sweetie shop for most of the journey.

As we travelled into the heart of Poland the contrast between affluent Germany and the poor Polish towns and cities was obvious. The farther east we drove, the more the places we passed through looked like the backdrop in old black and white spy movies. When we reached Warsaw it was hard not to picture the German Army marching through the streets. More than fifty years after World War Two, the memory of the Warsaw Ghetto I had read about in books still seemed quite vivid.

We arrived at the huge bus station and the passengers slowly made their way off, our muscles aching and legs stiff. I looked around the bustling depot wondering where to go from here. I collected my bags from the hold and, while the rest of the commuters met family and friends or purposefully made their way to their next destination, I wandered about in bewilderment. The planning stage had taken me as far as Warsaw. I knew I had to reach Warsaw Central Railway Station but where that might be I had no idea.

I stopped a few people and asked if they understood English but the blank stares in return gave me the answer. I approached various members of railway staff milling around the platforms but I was met with the same muted response. Then I spotted a small office with what appeared to be timetables in the window. It must be the ticket centre. I went in and asked the young woman behind the counter my standard question, "Do you speak English?"

"A little," she replied.

I couldn't believe it. Finally I was able to communicate with someone. I asked her if the international trains left from Warsaw

Central and if so, how did I get there? She confirmed it did and told me I should take one of the trams that left across the road from the bus station. She said any tram would do but first I must buy a ticket from the kiosk in the street.

I went outside and spotted the kiosk the lady had mentioned. I held out some Polish coins I'd received in my change at the roadside diner and pointed towards a tram. The attendant lifted some coins from my palm and gave me a ticket, and I tried out the Polish phrase I learned on the bus from London, "dziekuja" (thank you), before rushing across the road to the waiting tram.

The stop was very busy and the tram was already mobbed. I would later learn this was typical of Eastern European public transport, so much so that the trams are known as Sardine Transporters. I had a rucksack on my back and a bag in my hand as I wriggled up the tram steps, with people on either side of me doing the same.

In my excitement at arriving in Warsaw, I had placed my wallet in the back pocket of my jeans rather than my inside jacket pocket after purchasing the tram ticket. As I struggled up the steps I felt a hand reaching into my back pocket.

Fortunately, because I was stretched forward at the time, the pocket of my denims was tight. That, coupled with my twisting around and shouts, made the thief run off. I doubt anyone nearby knew what had happened. In fact, they probably wondered why this crazy man in their midst was squirming and shouting in a foreign language! I was lucky. All my cash and credit cards were in the wallet. You live and learn, and there was no more back pocket use for me.

Peering out the grimy windows between the heads and shoulders of my fellow sardines, I caught a glimpse of what I thought

was the train station. The tram pulled up at a stop and I followed others shuffling through the tight space to the exit, happy to be escaping the claustrophobic surroundings. I stood on the pavement and looked across the wide, bustling road at the railway station.

Between my destination and I there were trams, buses, cars and trucks going in every direction, with horns beeping and engines roaring. I didn't fancy my chances of making it across in one piece. Then I spotted the underpass. This will be easier, I thought, as I made my way down the stairs. However, when I reached the bottom I didn't find a corridor taking me under the road. Instead, it was a vast space that resembled an underground shopping mall: there were stores, restaurants and snack bars, with direction signs pointing towards the copious passageways and staircases. These signs, of course, were all in Polish. It was like I'd stumbled into the Tardis.

I surveyed my surroundings and tried to judge which of the corridors would lead me closest to the station. I picked a passageway that immediately turned left, then right and right again, and then upstairs to the street. When I reached the top I looked around for the station. I was farther away now than when I started!

Dejected and frustrated I made my way back down and into the bustling underground mall. I wondered if my train to Ukraine had departed already. I had no idea when it was due, but what if it left while I was stumbling around this concrete maze? I felt like an alien. How simple it would have been had I just understood the language.

I studied my options again and tried to determine which twisting passageway would lead me to the station. After a few moments I rolled the proverbial dice, hoping I would land on a ladder rather than another snake. As I reached the top of the steps I breathed a sigh of relief when the station came into view. This time I was on the correct side of the road.

Entering the concourse, I realised I wasn't home and dry quite yet. It was a massive, high structure and I had no clue where and how to buy a ticket. I walked over to the huge destination board and strained my neck to look at the scores of place names listed. There were several Polish towns, most of them new to me, and then a number of European place names: Berlin, Paris, Amsterdam, Moscow, Minsk. This was not Glasgow Central Station, that's for sure.

And then there it was among the scroll of destinations: Kiev, 21.00hrs. I still had time to spare. Each booth at the ticket office had a different list of place names taped to the window. I read through the destinations until I located Kiev and joined the short queue, feeling a little more relaxed.

When I reached the front I said in my best Russian, "I want a ticket to Kiev, please." The ticket seller replied in Polish. I had no idea what she'd said. I tried asking in English, but now she couldn't understand me. I didn't know what to do. I assumed my Russian would be understood in Poland but in retrospect it was foolish to think so. Desperation was beginning to set in when I heard a female voice behind me ask in English, "Can I help you?"

I looked round and found a young woman standing there.

"Do you speak English?" I asked, my voice peppered with hope, relief and joy.

"You want to travel to Kiev?" she asked me in her heavy accent. "I'm going to Kiev, too. We should travel together."

I stood beside her as she asked in Polish, I believe, for two tickets to Kiev. I was so grateful that she had come to my rescue.

She introduced herself as Tanya, a student returning home to Odessa after visiting friends in Poland. She told me our train journey was a long haul, over twenty-four hours, so suggested we buy some provisions for the trip. I watched over her luggage while she purchased some food and drink, and then we made our way to the platform.

The train was so huge that I couldn't see where it began. It consisted of at least twenty carriages. We stepped inside and made our way through the narrow corridors as we tried to locate our sleeper compartment. It was an old-fashioned and quite primitive train, typical of Eastern European transportation. For example, at the end of each carriage was the toilet, where the metal pan had a hole at the bottom and the waste dropped straight onto the track. I wouldn't like to have had the job of maintaining the railway lines in Poland, that's for sure.

We located our sleeper compartment, a poky, tight space with four bunks – two on each side, one above the other. I soon learned we were cohabiting with two men, aged around thirty, who were also travelling together. It was a rather tight space for four adults to share for so many hours and I prepared myself for a long, awkward trip. Everything was a new and strange experience for me. I wondered what was next.

The train ride was much better than I expected, though, and this was thanks to Tanya. She was a super girl and we chatted for hours. I explained to her why I was travelling to Kiev and she translated for the two men. It took a long time to conduct a conversation with the multi-way, multi-lingual dialogue, but then we had plenty of it to kill.

When we weren't talking I gazed out the window at the passing landscapes of industrial estates, sprawling cities, grey towns and rolling green hills. I dozed intermittently before finally falling off to sleep.

I woke with a start. We were in darkness. As my senses returned I realised the train was at a standstill. Then I noticed the noise, the loud clanking, that had stirred me. I sat up and pulled back the window blind. The bright light illuminating the scene dazzled my eyes but as they focused I saw a three-storey building, painted green, with a metal staircase running up the outside. There were lots of men shouting to be heard over the heavy banging. Powerful white lights on poles lighted the whole area. It was like an image from a James Bond movie.

My mind raced as quickly as my heart thumped. I feared all of the passengers would be led off the train and into this building for some kind of security procedure or intense questioning. The angry shouting continued. Maybe that was the first of the passengers being led off against their will. Whatever was happening, I decided it couldn't be good.

"Tanya," I whispered. "Tanya, what's going on?"

I heard her stirring and turning over in her bunk. She muttered something in a mixture of English and Russian but she was obviously still half sleeping and I couldn't make head or tail of her explanation. She fell back asleep while I continued to squint out the gap in the blinds, careful not to draw unwanted attention to our compartment.

I remained rigid in my bunk, listening to the noises and imagining increasingly wicked and worrying outcomes to this halt in the journey. I waited and waited, half expecting the door to burst open at any moment and police or security or officials or...

somebody to pull us out of the darkness towards the spotlights and into the green building.

After what must have been at least two hours, the train started up and slowly began moving again, rolling into the black of night much to my relief. I laid my head down and attempted to relax but it took a while before I calmed down and was able to drift off to sleep.

The next morning I again asked Tanya if she had any idea what had happened during the night. This time I could understand. Apparently Russian train tracks are farther apart than those in other parts of Europe, so the train has to be stopped, jacked up and fitted with different axle assemblies and bogie wheels to fit the Russian lines. So the brightly lit James Bond set was, in actuality, a giant railway shed!

As the train swept into Ukraine and that scare faded into the distance, my next nervy moment was quickly upon me. We could hear firm knocks on the doors of nearby sleeper compartments followed by brief chat. Tanya said it would be the customs and security control, and sure enough when the door opened two stern faced, uniformed officials faced us. My familiarity with spy movies was beginning to become an unwanted distraction, because now I sat in my bunk fearing I was about to be discovered by the government police. Discovered doing what I wasn't sure, but coming from the west I found the whole procedure unsettling and I worried whether or not my papers were in order and if my luggage contravened any rules or regulations of which I was unaware.

The day before, when the Polish Border Guards checked our papers, Tanya seemed quite tense. But this time she was completely relaxed in the face of these military-types as they asked a series of questions to each of us in the compartment. I, of course, had no clue what was being said so thank goodness for Tanya, who translated. I was asked to fill in a foreign entry form, which in these days was printed only in Russian, no English version. Without her I would have been unable to complete it. The guards also asked me how much money I carried, which I thought was a little strange. I was honest about the amount and it seemed to be ok, because they returned my passport and moved on to the next cabin.

Finally we pulled into Kiev and the vast concourse of the railway station. It was a contrast to the tiny compartment that afforded no privacy. Tanya stuck by me and asked where I was meeting my friend. I explained Anatoli didn't know I was coming but I intended to call him now that I had arrived.

Tanya said she would call Anatoli on my behalf before she left to catch her connecting train to Odessa, but when she called from the payphone there was no answer at his house. I had one other number I could try, a friend of Anatoli who also lived in Kiev. I had never met him but perhaps he could contact Anatoli to let him know I was here. Tanya called the number and thankfully someone picked up.

After a brief conversation she hung up the receiver and took me to the station's waiting room, where she said someone called Andre would collect me. With that we said our goodbyes and I thanked her for her help and for providing company on the long trip. And then Tanya from Odessa was gone.

I still think about Tanya occasionally today, because without her it's unlikely I would have made it beyond Poland on the first trip. Perhaps I would have turned back and never attempted to travel to Ukraine again. I wish I'd taken a picture of us together,

Jim chats with an interested passer by at an early vigil in George Square, Glasgow.

Jim gives Margaret a kiss goodbye as he sets off for EuroDisney, with his mum (blue shellsuit) and daughter (white overcoat) amongst the onlookers.

Almost there. Jim stops for a rest at a junction in France.

After an eventful journey that saw him robbed and knocked down, Jim finally makes it to EuroDisney.

Laden down with as many bags as he can carry, Jim sets off on another long trip to Ukraine.

KYIV-ZHYTOMYR-RIVNE-LVIV
LILLE-REIMS-METZ-PARIS, ANTWERPEN-
BRUXELLES-MONS-LIEGE, ZVOLEN-BRATISLAVA

The basic bus that takes Jim from Kiev to Brussels on the long road home.

Малин

Welcome to Malin.

An archaic ambulance pulls into Malin Hospital. The ambulances in the Malin area have little medical equipment inside.

My good friend Anatoli Artemenko, without whom my Ukraine trips wouldn't be possible, clutches two hugely dedicated doctors, Dr Angela (left) and Dr Victoria (right).

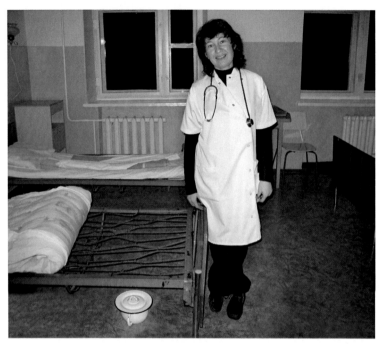

The dedicated Dr Victoria poses beside a rusty bed frame and a thin, stained mattress. Bedpans are still a familiar sight in this hospital.

Pots containing who knows what in the makeshift kitchen in the children's ward.

A typical scene in the hospital's children's ward: broken furniture and flimsy beds.

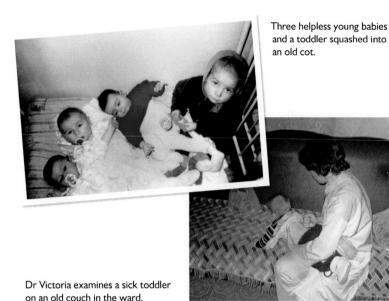

Three helpless young babies
and a toddler squashed into
an old cot.

Dr Victoria examines a sick toddler
on an old couch in the ward.

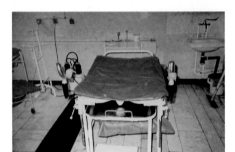

Equipment from the hospital's
maternity unit.

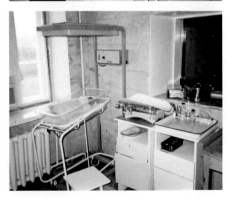

A newborn baby wrapped in
blankets, placed under a broken
heat lamp.

A well deserved break for Dr Victoria (far left), Dr Angela (far right) and two colleagues.

Worried parents sit with their sick son. Note the thin mattress on the bed.

A sick boy sits on mismatched bed linen.

Taking this sneaky picture of the bank teller converting Jim's money almost resulted in him and Anatoli being ejected from the bank by furious security.

A happy Jim poses with the Ukrainian money. Now it's time to buy supplies for the hospital.

Dr Victoria purchases a carpet for the newly created children's playroom.

Dr Victoria sorts through recently bought supplies, including a new computer, microwave and pots. Note the toilet rolls and cleaning fluids – even these basics have to be purchased by Jim.

but my camera was at the bottom of my rucksack. Now I always make sure to have my digital camera close to hand, as I never know when it might be needed.

I stood in the waiting room, a huge space that was bathed in the winter sunlight thanks to its beautiful domed roof. Gazing around I spotted many military officers standing at attention and intently watching those of us who were milling about. Their very presence was intimidating, despite the curious sight of the large brimmed hats they wore that appeared to be too big for their heads. Would they question me? If so, how should I respond – in English or might I attempt Russian? I thought of spy movies again and felt like I was waiting to make a bag switch with a contact.

Time was moving on. I had waited a while now. Questions were racing through my head: how would Andre find me in this place? He didn't know what I looked like. What if he never came? How could I find Anatoli? Maybe he had been called away on business suddenly and wouldn't be home for days. Perhaps I should have told him I was coming.

I had no mobile phone, no Ukrainian money and no Tanya.

I waited and waited, but still nothing. Maybe Andre had been here and I'd missed him. But how would I know when I had no idea what he looked like? Then again, how would he find me? There were lots of travellers passing through the waiting room.

While I continued to worry I noticed a young man across the room holding up a large piece of torn cardboard. There was something written on it. I moved closer and tried to decipher the scrawled words. It appeared to read "Gem Dxeeles". Could it be?

I hurried over to the man and said, "Andre, Tanya, telefone?"

"Da," he replied, and indicated I should follow him.

We left the railway station and walked towards a battered Lada car, where another man sat in the driver's seat. Andre motioned for me to go inside. I went into the backseat while these two strangers sat before me, clearly unable to speak English. All sorts of thoughts and scenarios were playing out in my mind but what could I do except trust that everything would be fine?

We drove in silence, travelling for some time before the driver pulled up beside a block of flats. Every sight we passed on the way had been an experience. It all looked so different here – the people, their clothes, the buildings, trams, streets and markets. Andre stepped from the car and indicated for me to follow. I scrambled out, clutching my rucksack and bag. Andre said something to the driver, and then the car sped off. What now, I thought.

We entered the flats through the rubbish-strewn entrance and got in a lift.

What is happening here? Is this where Anatoli lives?

We came out the lift and Andre opened an apartment door. It was clean and tidy, although somewhat old fashioned to my western eyes. A woman stood in the hallway, ready to greet us. I presumed it was Andre's wife.

"Borsch?" she asked, looking at me.

"Da, pashalasta," I replied. (Yes, thank you.) I sat down at their table for my bowl of soup and bread, followed by a cup of tea. I tried out some Russian words and phrases I knew while I ate. They smiled but obviously didn't understand my pronunciation. I could tell they were nice, friendly folk, despite the language barrier. I gifted them a picture book about Scotland to thank them for their hospitality.

"Anatoli?" I asked, pointing to the clock on the wall.

Andre held up two fingers, which I assumed meant two hours.

About an hour later, however, the doorbell interrupted the silence and thankfully it was my friend.

"Jim!" he exclaimed. "When did you arrive in Kiev? You never told me you were coming?"

I told him that the last time I called he'd mentioned he was going to Germany in a few months' time. So since I had all the letters and documentation, I thought I would come over and surprise him. In retrospect that was probably a mistake.

"You told me to come over anytime," I smiled.

Anatoli laughed and said we should be on our way, as we would soon be competing with the rush hour traffic. I thanked Andre and his wife for their hospitality, and then embarked on the next leg of my mammoth journey.

I told Anatoli all about my trip so far while we travelled across the city to his apartment. When I left Scotland I had no idea the difficulties I would encounter in trying to reach Eastern Europe. But here I was, taking the Metro and tram through Kiev while thousands of workers made their way home. Standing on a packed carriage I realised the Sardine Transporter wasn't unique to Poland. I felt it was an achievement in making it this far, albeit with one or two stumbles along the way.

When we reached his flat I was introduced to Anatoli's wife Elena, their 17-year-old daughter Maria, and Elena's mother Riasa, who also lived with them. While Anatoli was of course fluent in English and his daughter had learned it at school, Elena could only understand a little but was unable to speak it. Riasa could only talk the language of her birth country, Russia.

I made a brief call home from Anatoli's phone. It was the first time I had called since I arrived in Ukraine, although I'd spoken to Margaret from London and also en route at motorway

83

services. But these were always very brief chats since I was afraid the bus would leave while I was in the phone box. The bus drivers didn't understand English, so I was unable to ask how long we would be stopped.

It had been a long and draining day and I was completely exhausted. That night was bliss as I slept in a proper bed for the first time in three days. It had never felt so good.

The following morning I felt revitalised and full of energy, especially when I remembered I was waking up in Ukraine. Anatoli called the children's ward before he left for work to tell them a gentleman called Jim Gillies had come from Scotland to visit the kids in their care. The nurse on the other end wrote down the details and said she would call back. When she did I was happy to hear from Anatoli that there were no problems. Not that there should have been, since I had already received an invitation from the hospital for the purposes of my visa application, but I was quickly learning that very little was straightforward in this country.

On weekdays Anatoli and Elena worked and Maria was at university, so rather than go out in Kiev alone, Anatoli advised me to stay indoors. He warned it wouldn't be safe to venture out by myself. This was quite an alarming caution and I wondered why he felt this way. He explained that since it was my first time in Kiev and I didn't know my way around and was unable to speak Ukrainian or Russian, should the police stop me I could be taken to a station for questioning. Apparently people could often be halted in the street as they went about their business, especially if they looked like they didn't belong there. This was due to the infamous security regulations of the notorious President Kuchma. Anatoli said that if I were taken to a police station, any discrepancies in my documents would be spotted. He emphasised my documents were fine, but the possibility of an overzealous official checking my visa, passport and signed letter of invitation from the hospital was best avoided.

Perhaps to stress the stranglehold the president had on his country and its people, Anatoli told me his political views – which suffice to say weren't in line with those of Kuchma – had led to his telephone being tapped. I learned over subsequent trips that many other journalists suffered the same intrusion during the Kuchma years. At the time of my first trip, Kuchma had just been re-elected for his second term. He was only the second president of independent Ukraine, and while he was credited with helping the economy grow and for improving relations between Ukraine and Russia, his time in charge was notable for corruption scandals and a tightening of the media's freedom of speech.

The time I did spend in Anatoli's house during the day was quite amusing, since it was just Riasa and I. She chatted away non-stop in her native tongue, while I tried to pick out a word or two in an attempt to follow her conversation. Any attempts I made to contribute were unsuccessful. We got on well despite the language barrier, a sentiment that would be repeated count-less times in the future with many Ukrainians and Russians I met.

On one of Anatoli's days off he took me on a trip to an or-phanage in Kiev along with a Belgian charity group. The condi-tions were horrendous. The children had a roof over their heads, but that was the only positive I could find. It was so sad seeing the deprived surroundings of the little boys and girls that some of our group couldn't handle it and went outside to cry. With that same group I visited the Exclusion Zone with Anatoli as our guide, a powerful and affecting trip that I will detail in a later chapter.

But there was only one reason I had travelled to Ukraine and that was to finally visit the children of Malin's hospital. That long awaited trip happened on my second day in the country. Unfortunately the mournful words and dire descriptions in Alexandr's faded letters were only a mild, understated description. The reality was even worse and the intervening years hadn't been kind.

It was an experience that was to change my life.

The Hospital

The day had finally arrived.

There were butterflies in my stomach and a dry lump in my throat as we made our way across Kiev to pick up Anatoli's minivan to begin the journey. This trip, much like the rest of my Ukrainian visit, would be a voyage into the unknown.

Eight years after receiving those quite unexpected letters from a stranger called Alexandr, begging me to help those poor children suffering in a hospital within a town I'd never heard of, I was now just a few hours from entering the place he wrote so much about.

I didn't know what to expect.

Just how bad would the conditions be? What would the doctors make of this foreigner coming to the hospital? Would I actually be able to do any good? The questions swirled round in my head like an eagle circling its prey as we made a two-hour journey by public transport – first a tram and then the Metro - just to reach Anatoli's vehicle. There is no parking available near the block of flats where Anatoli lives so he keeps his minivan in a lock up, since he tends to use public transport to make his way round Kiev.

Joining us on the trip to the hospital was one of Anatoli's best friends, Grigori Babachuk, who just so happens to be a renowned artist. We headed northwest towards rural Ukraine, passing by imposing, looming factories, open farmland, and houses of all shapes, sizes and conditions. As we whizzed along straight, fast stretches of road, we drove by cyclists, walkers and traditional horses and carts. I had that feeling again of walking onto the set of an old black and white movie. It was like another planet. I had to remind myself the world was on the cusp of the millennium.

But while I was engrossed by the strange landscape all around me, Anatoli had spotted something more sinister in his rear view mirror and was now deep in conversation with Grigori. "There's a police car following us, Jim. It has been since we left Kiev," Anatoli explained. He didn't sound too concerned, in fact he was quite nonchalant about it. I, on the other hand, was shocked.

I had found it hard to comprehend the news from the day before, not only that Anatoli's phone line was tapped but that the police had been to the hospital to inquire about my visit. But to now actually be followed as we went to visit some underprivileged and sick kids was unbelievable.

The police car remained at a distance, at times disappearing from view. Just when I thought it might have gone and the officers had found something better to do, the car reappeared and continued to follow us.

We turned off the main roads onto narrow minor streets as we passed through small towns with strange sounding names, like Baradanka, that I struggled to pronounce. There were traders standing on the roadside there selling all manner of items. As we drove slowly by I watched a woman purchase a large, live fish from what appeared to be a blue storage box filled with water. The trader put the fish on weighing scales but it flopped off and onto the ground, where it squirmed and writhed. He picked it back up, sloshed it in the water, and returned it to the scales. He then handed the fish to the woman, who dropped her dinner into a carrier bag. As she paid for her purchase and walked away I could see the fish was still moving, its tail and head flapping against the plastic. Another planet indeed.

The police car continued to be visible in the van's mirrors. While I thought it was worrying to be in a country where ordinary people were placed under such surveillance, Anatoli and Grigori were amused by it, shrugging their shoulders and saying such things happened in Ukraine. I suppose having lived through Soviet times they would have experienced a lot worse.

A short distance along the road, Anatoli pulled up at a splintered wooden road sign. "That says Malin in Russian," he told me. "Now we just have to find the hospital." The police car finally ceased following us here, perhaps satisfied that we were just going to the hospital and didn't have more sinister intentions, whatever they might be.

Anatoli had done well to find the town, considering he'd never been here before and had to contend with the distraction of the police tail, no matter how little he said their presence failed to bother him.

We drove past picturesque houses with pretty gardens and into the town centre. I was able to read some Cyrillic names on the buildings, such as bank, hotel and shop. However, I would never have been able to ask for directions to the hospital, which is what Anatoli and Grigori had to do as we approached some locals. It reminded me how much I was indebted to Anatoli; without him I would never have been able to make the trip.

According to the instructions we would be at the hospital within minutes, as it was only two miles from the town centre. After a short drive we turned a corner and Anatoli pointed towards a large, flat roofed building and said, "There it is, Jim".

At first I thought it was an old 1950s style office block. It was a cold, grey, uninviting looking structure. There was no car park so we parked the minivan alongside some other cars in front of the entrance. As I got out of the passenger side I spotted an archaic ambulance nearby. It looked like an old beat up Volkswagen camper van. I walked over and peered through the windows. An ancient metal stretcher and torn padded mattress were the only things I could see in the rear; there was no medical equipment visible. I walked round to the front and looked through the cracked windscreen, where I could see the driver and passenger seats were ripped and noticeably loose from their mountings. The vehicle should have been in a museum, but instead it was in daily use. What a contrast to the state-of-the-art vehicles in the UK. I wondered if this was the only type of ambulance at the hospital's disposal.

I later learned that the hospital served thirty thousand people. However, it doesn't have a casualty ward. Apparently in wintry weather, when the road conditions are poor, many pregnant mothers lose their babies due to the lack of life-saving equipment in Malin hospital. As far as I am aware, if a patient arrives requiring emergency treatment they have to be taken to another hospital in the Zhitomir region. I hope they don't have to depend on that clapped out ambulance to take them there.

We walked towards the entrance doors of the six-storey hospital, the very image discouraging. Now that I was closer I decided it looked more like an abandoned factory than an office block.

I took a deep, nervous breath as we stepped inside.

Sadly it wasn't just the exterior that resembled an abandoned factory. There was no reception desk or hospital shop here, none of the hustle and bustle expected of a busy hospital. Anatoli stopped a passing woman wearing a white coat and asked her where the children's ward was located. She pointed towards the staircase. It was on the third floor.

We took care as we walked up the worn flights of stairs because they were chipped, broken and uneven, and we were careful not to grip too tightly on the loose, shaky banisters. Many of the light fittings overhead were broken.

We reached the third floor, where there was an open area, like a waiting room except there were no chairs. We pushed through a door that led into a long corridor lined by draughty windows, where the wind whistled a dull, monotonous drone.

Finally I was here. I was actually in the children's department that Alexandr had written about. I could feel the excitement building within me, yet at the same time the awful conditions were causing a great deal of consternation.

A nurse in uniform wearing an old-fashioned tall white hat was perched at a desk filling in paperwork, while two small children stood at her side watching her every move. Their appearance and behaviour would soon become a familiar one to me: the happy but pale faces, the black circles framing their innocent eyes, and their polite and unselfish manner.

The nurse looked up from her handwritten notes – there was not a computer in sight – and spoke to Anatoli and Grigori.

Afterwards she made a call and then led us into an office with a cracked glass panelled door, where we were asked to wait.

After a few minutes the door opened and the nurse returned, followed by a line of doctors and nurses. Anatoli acted as translator while the introductions were made. They seemed pleased to meet me.

A doctor explained they wanted us to join them for lunch in the staff room. Over the meal I explained about the letters from Alexandr requesting my help, about his sister working as a nurse at the hospital, and my quest to come to Ukraine to try to help the children in the ward. They remembered giving Alexandr the wish list he had sent, but they lost contact with him after his sister left her job.

I hadn't wanted to arrive at the hospital empty handed, because that would have made the trip rather futile. Unfortunately it was a difficult financial time for our family, but I did manage to scrape together £100 of my own money to give to the doctors. It was all I could afford on top of my travel costs. I have always made sure to pay every penny of my expenses from my own pocket, with the help of Margaret. Every pound donated to the appeal has gone directly to help the kids in the hospital.

I handed the cash to one of the doctors. I don't think they had ever received money in such a manner before, but they were very delighted to accept it. They could not believe a man had travelled by bus from Scotland to give them £100 of his own savings. A doctor asked me about the Ukrainian link in my family background. When I said there was none, that I just wanted to help, she seemed surprised.

Another doctor explained that due to the inheritance of the Chernobyl legacy, many of the children passing through the ward's doors have immune system deficiencies, bronchitis, thyroid gland problems including thyroid cancer and diseases of the kidney and spleen, and growth deformities. Yet because the hospital is situated in zone four of the exclusion zone it receives very little financial support from the government.

Some sick kids are brought to the hospital for treatment by their worried parents, but their desperation only grows because they have no money to pay for the medicine that would help their child. Other parents abandon their babies and children at the hospital in the misguided hope that the treatment they cannot afford to pay will be provided by the doctors. If the doctors had the resources at their disposal, I have no doubt they would, but sadly this is not the case. Then there are the orphans cared for by the hospital until they are old enough to be taken to a state orphanage.

The principal doctor, Victoria Baklanova, took Anatoli, Grigori and I on a tour of the ward.

Nothing could have prepared me for what I saw.

Despite it being a children's ward there was no playroom. There were no toys to be found, no posters on the walls, no bright colours to cheer up the sick kids. I soon learned this was the least of the place's problems.

It wasn't so much a ward as a series of rooms with beds, because there was almost no medical equipment to be seen. The sparse apparatus they did have was broken, obsolete or both.

I was shocked to see babies lying on stained mattresses in old, rusted metal cots with peeling paint. Dr Victoria pulled at the loose sidebars of the collapsing structure and showed the space that a baby could easily fall through. The toddlers and older kids, some were in their teenage years, had to make do with ancient metal bed frames with broken headboards. The adjacent bedside cabinets were dilapidated.

As we moved from room to room I just couldn't comprehend what I was seeing. It was Dickensian conditions.

The paint on the blue walls flaked and large sections of fallen plaster exposed the ceiling. The lights were broken, the glass on the windows was smashed or cracked, and drafts blew in through the worn frames.

The bare wooden floors were scraped and splintering. They were washed with just wet rags and mops.

The sinks had no hot running water, the toilets had no seats, and buckets were provided for the used toilet paper because the flushing mechanisms were so poor.

The one Victorian-style bath that they used to wash the children was held up by bricks to stabilise the plumbing around its base.

They had a kitchen on the ward. Well, a room with an old cooker, fridge and some pots and pans missing their handles. There was a major problem with rats and mice in this room, as was indicated by the holes in the floor and in the corner of the tiled wall around the sink's rusted pipes.

Unlike hospitals at home, no meals are provided for the patients. So some mothers stay in the hospital and prepare food for their children. One mum there at the time told us her husband had recently made his way on bicycle and foot through poor weather from their village ten miles away, just to bring food for his little boy. The doctors and nurses feed those babies and kids without parental care as best they can manage in the trying circumstances. Again, it was such a contrast to what I was used to in British hospitals.

I was taken to a room where three pale-faced fourteen-year-old boys sat on the frayed sheets of their beds. Each had pneumonia, but there was insufficient medicine to treat them. Another room had a wee boy of around seven years of age lying in a dilapidated bed, hooked up to a drip bottle that hung from a shaky stand. His mother sat in front of a cracked window, holding his hand. Dr Victoria explained he had a problem with his kidneys, but the staff was doing all they could for him within their limited resources.

Anatoli told the boy's mother why I was there. It was a humbling experience, the first of many, when she thanked me for coming to Malin to help her son.

Dr Victoria asked the three of us if we would like to accompany her to the town's pharmacy to buy some items using the money I had donated.

As we made our way out of the hospital I was still trying to digest what I had witnessed.

I just could not comprehend the scenes of utter deprivation and poverty. It was obvious the doctors and nurses were committed to their jobs and to the children, despite being forced to operate in such depressing working conditions and with an inefficient level of medical provisions. I was appalled and really upset by what I saw inside. The comments passed on from Alexandr's sister in the letters hadn't prepared me for the shocking set-up.

The four of us made our way to the local bank in town to change the £100 into Ukrainian Hryvnia, and then onto the pharmacy. The pharmacist must have been quite perturbed to see a doctor from the hospital come into her store with three strange men, one a foreigner who couldn't speak a word of the language. When the situation was explained, she invited us into her office for tea and biscuits. We also had a glass of a very strong tasting non-alcoholic drink produced locally. It was safe to say this was a little different from a visit to the chemist in the UK. While we had our refreshments, Dr Victoria and the pharmacist collected the medicines purchased with the money and stacked them into boxes.

Before we returned to the hospital we bought powdered baby milk, food and other supplies for the children from a shop. I made sure to obtain receipts for everything purchased. They were handwritten in Ukrainian but Anatoli looked them over and assured me all was in order.

I'll never forget the moment back in the ward later that day, as a nurse fed an abandoned baby. "Look Jim," Dr Victoria said. "That baby is being fed with the milk powder bought with your money."

I had hit it off with Victoria straight away, despite the language barrier. She is a very nice woman and a good doctor held in high regard by her colleagues. We quickly became friends during this first meeting and it's a friendship that has endured.

By the time I left the ward I was glad, despite the harrowing scenes, to have made the two thousand mile, three-day bus journey to the hospital.

I had seen the poorly children with smiles on their white faces despite their suffering. I watched mothers fraught with worry as they sat helplessly at bedsides. I met the wonderfully caring doctors and nurses doing their best with very little money. And I viewed the broken, obsolete medical equipment.

It had been a poignant experience.

I felt I had formed a bond of friendship with the people I'd met. It was just one day but that was enough for me to plainly see the hospital desperately needed much more help than I had been able to give on this occasion.

As we waved goodbye to the doctors, nurses, mothers and children, I knew this couldn't be a one-off trip.

I made a promise to myself to do whatever I could to continue trying to help. I was already planning ahead. By the end of my first Ukrainian adventure Anatoli, on my behalf, had made several calls to Dr Victoria to note a list of future needs.

Now that I had been to Malin hospital once, I knew I had to return. And that's exactly what I have done year after year ever since.

Little by Little

If the Chernobyl disaster and its victims' plight had occupied my thoughts before, now that I had seen the dismal reality with my own eyes it became an obsession.

I couldn't stop telling folk about what I had witnessed in Ukraine. About the kindness and friendliness of the people despite the despondent situation they were in through no fault of their own. Good people who were forced to endure terrible hardships, ill health and abject poverty. But most of all, the poor, sick children living like hobos in Malin Hospital.

I had a new purpose in life.

I don't know if Margaret and the rest of my family thought before I went to Kiev and Malin that the trip would be a one-off to satisfy my interest and to offer a small token gesture of help. But now that I was home I was more determined than ever to bring change and attention to the Chernobyl victims.

I couldn't do it all, but I could focus on a small part of the problem. I now knew just how bad things were in Malin's hospital. I understood, and was overawed, by how much the doctors required to help the kids.

I told my family that the hospital children had never received any outside care, so I had to do my best to provide it. They joked that I was a man on a mission, but they knew I was resolutely determined and serious about carrying on with what I had begun.

But where to start?

The children's ward had nothing. They needed so much but I had no idea how to get it for them. I would spend countless hours on the phone, going through the Yellow Pages and calling medical supplies companies. I didn't know where else to start but this idea turned out to be a complete waste of time. On every occasion I called one of these companies I was met with what quickly became a familiar stock of responses.

The person who would deal with your inquiry is – delete as appropriate - out of the office, in a meeting, on holiday. When I called back they were still unavailable, no matter the time of day.

Another favourite response was, are you a registered charity? Or we can't help due to health and safety regulations.

Call our head office in England. When I did I was given a similar knockback or told to put my request in writing. That was just a waste of a stamp.

We only work with a nominated charity.

Our company receives many such requests, I'm afraid we can't help them all.

I was banging my head against a wall. I had no doubt that what many of the companies were telling me may have been true but that was of little comfort. But I had to keep trying no matter how many times I was told, "Sorry, we can't help".

I would inform whomever I spoke with about the plight of the children in Malin in the hope it would perhaps inspire them to make more of an effort to help. Unfortunately this was never the case. One large medical company has a depot near my home in Cumbernauld and after making contact with them they seemed to be a good prospect to aid my efforts. I visited the local depot three times and contacted their head office in England, hopeful of a positive outcome. I really thought I would get something from them. In the end all I got was the run around.

I was staying in touch with Anatoli during all of this and I told him I planned on returning to Ukraine before the end of the year. So in November 1999, eight months after my first visit, I travelled to Kiev using the same transportation and route as before. I wasn't completely empty-handed. A district nurse friend had provided me with some surplus supplies such as bandages, surgical gowns and disposable syringes. It wasn't much but at least it was a start. Once again I also gave the doctors some money to buy a few essentials.

During this second trip I became more familiar with my host Anatoli and his family and friends, with my surroundings in Kiev, and with the hard-working and resolute doctors and nurses (especially Dr Victoria, who was becoming a good friend). Unfortunately my second viewing of the children's ward in Malin Hospital only confirmed my reaction from the first time: that the good natured but sick and abandoned kids deserved, and more importantly desperately needed, so much more.

Back home I continued to throw myself into finding a way to help the hospital. Any spare moment was spent on what was becoming my other life on the opposite side of the continent. Whether it was attempting to secure equipment and supplies for the ward, organising the vigil, taking Russian language night classes, fundraising or reading up on the details of the Chernobyl disaster and Ukrainian politics, I was totally focused on the task at hand.

I thought I had finally made a breakthrough when an old friend contacted me to say she could provide some medical stock for the Malin children. I was delighted. Marion Scott and her husband have been friends with Margaret and I for many years, dating back to when our children went to school together. She worked in an administration office in Glasgow's Royal Infirmary and said she would ask around to see if anyone could help. A while later she called to say the hospital store in the grounds, where all the Infirmary's medical supplies were issued, had some items surplus to requirement that I could gladly have. What brilliant news.

I went to the hospital the following day and was taken to the store. I was expecting to be handed a couple of carrier bags of goods, so I could barely believe it when the storeman showed me two pallets piled high. Scribbled on many of the boxes and packaging were messages such as "To help the Chernobyl kids".

I had a problem. And not the usual one. Instead of having very little supplies to take to Dr Victoria I now had a mountain of goods that I had no way of transporting. The staff at the Infirmary store presumed I had a lorry or van parked outside that I could load up and then drive to Ukraine. But I explained that I travelled by public transport and, although I had by now discovered a once-a-week London to Kiev coach from Eastern European Buses that made the trip a little easier if not shorter, I could only take with me what I could carry in my two large holdalls.

I said I would call the bus company and ask if they might make an exception with their bag limits and transport the supplies for me, but sadly the coach manager said it wouldn't be possible. I called a few other bus companies that travelled across Europe but inevitably they all told me the same.

So I went back to the Infirmary stores and took as much as I thought I could possibly stuff into my bags. I thanked the staff at the Infirmary for their kind consideration and contribution, but having to leave the piles of desperately-needed supplies behind made me so upset. I felt sad when I arrived at Malin Hospital and saw how happy the doctors were to receive the small amount I had brought. In my mind's eye I saw multiples of what I had delivered sitting on pallets in Glasgow, personally addressed to the kids in the hospital.

Slowly, however, I made my way through those pallets, bringing the supplies over in small amounts over the course of a few years. By 2006 the hospital stores for the west of Scotland had been centralised to Larkhall in Lanarkshire and the donations came to an end, despite my appeals to the new distribution centre.

My friendship with Marion led her to introduce me to a colleague who was interested in my appeal. Colin Chitty was the fundraising director of the Royal Infirmary Appeals Trust and he said he could provide a number of hospital beds and bedside lockers from the old accident and emergency unit. A new casualty department had just opened at the Infirmary and was fitted with new furnishings, so the old ones were only going to be thrown away should I not want them. Of course I did, the beds and lockers in the kids' ward were crumbling, rusting and dilapidated. But there was no way these were fitting in my holdalls. I needed a lorry.

I contacted countless transport companies and haulage firms, but none were able to deliver the beds to Ukraine. I asked my employer at the time, Romec, which had plenty of large vehicles, if they might be able to assist. But again my pleas were to no avail. I even made an appeal to truck drivers through the pages of a national newspaper but received no response.

One transport manager from a trucking company told me that although his business took goods to Europe they didn't deliver or pass through Ukraine because entering the country required much more documentation and truck licensing papers than in other countries. It appeared that the red tape of Ukraine was curtailing my efforts once again. Unfortunately this wouldn't be the last time. It was becoming apparent that bureaucracy had no interest in helping sick children.

After about six weeks of frustration, Colin told me the beds were occupying space that was now required and if I couldn't take them one of the nurses involved in a Romania appeal would. I had tried my best but I was getting nowhere, so I told Colin to give them to the nurse. I felt I had failed again. It was maddening.

On three of my last four visits to Ukraine I have gone to a local furniture store in Malin with Dr Victoria to purchase new beds for the hospital. So far we have bought twelve beds and three cots, and hopefully I can add to this in future trips. But if only I had found transportation for the Infirmary's beds the money could have spent on some other necessities.

It's tough knowing how much medical equipment the children's ward needs yet being able to do little about it. I had asked Dr Victoria to give me a list of items they required but sadly most of the apparatus is far beyond the means my yearly budget can usually stretch. However, on one occasion I was able to buy a lifesaving machine thanks to an amazing response from big-hearted individuals who read about my work in Malin.

After finishing work in Glasgow city centre one afternoon in 2003, I decided to drop into the nearby Sunday Post offices.

The paper had always been in our house as I grew up and it was known for its human-interest stories and for being a family newspaper. I thought, with that being the case, there might be some interest in what I was trying to do for disadvantaged kids in another country. An article appeared in the Post soon afterwards, complete with my postal address.

Within a few days letters began falling through the letterbox from readers. My story really seemed to have struck a chord with them. "I think it is wonderful that you think of others, unlike a lot of people who only think of themselves," wrote one lady. She also enclosed a donation. So did many others. Every day for a couple of weeks at least one letter was delivered containing a kind message and generous contribution. One of those who gave money was a retired miner in England, who sent me a three figure contribution and has continued to send regular donations ever since.

A number of weeks after the article appeared the postman pushed a thick brown jiffy bag through the letterbox. Margaret picked it up and commented that it was unlikely to be from any of the newspaper readers since so much time had passed since the article was printed. I told her to open it and as she ripped the envelope a piece of paper fell out with the words, "For your children", written on it. Inside the jiffy bag was a thick wad of bank notes. I pulled them out and started counting, scarcely able to believe what I was seeing. It came to £3000. Absolutely incredible. I looked at the jiffy bag again; it was sent with just a normal stamp, not even registered. What if the envelope had gone missing in the mail? I shuddered even thinking about it.

I couldn't believe that someone would be so generous and selfless as to send an anonymous note with such a huge sum of money. I have never been able to say thank you to the person responsible, but hopefully he or she knows how greatly appreciated it was and the impact it had on Malin hospital.

In total the newspaper readers had donated £5000. Thanks to other donations and fundraising efforts over the course of the year I carried £7200 with me on my next trip to the hospital; my greatest ever total. The doctors were amazed when I presented them with the wad of Scottish and English banknotes. The local bank was equally ruffled and for a while it looked like we might have some problems converting the money, because the bank was simply not used to handling such large amounts of cash. Thankfully the problem was overcome and Dr Victoria had a large pile of hryvnia to do with what she wished. I knew what most of the cash would be spent on. Now the hospital could finally purchase a resuscitation unit for the maternity ward.

I hadn't spent quite so much time in the maternity ward as I had the children's, but I was aware the problems were just as pronounced there. Indeed they were throughout the hospital. Nurses and health officials I had come into contact with at home had asked in disbelief how a maternity unit could survive without a resuscitation unit? Well, now they would no longer have to cope because they could buy one of the £4000 machines.

By the time I next returned to Malin the unit had been in place for six months and had already saved the lives of fifteen babies. I was so happy to hear the news but I couldn't help but think of the number of poorly babies that were unlucky to have been born prior to its purchase.

Touching and emotional experiences at the hospital have only made me more determined to help the doctors and young patients.

One afternoon during a visit to the children's ward I was shown the "hospital pets". Inside a large glass jar, half filled with straw and its lid punctured with air holes, were three mice. The jar was kept in one of the rooms with the sick kids, who were thrilled to have the pets despite the crude nature of the well-intentioned gesture.

On another trip a young English teacher from the local school had agreed to be my translator for the day. After an hour of being by my side Ludmilla asked if I would mind if she could take a moment to visit her son, who was a patient. I had no idea.

"Of course", I told her. "You don't need to ask. It's more important to see your sick son than help me." It puzzled me a little as to why she would even feel the need to ask, but the Ukrainian people are so selfless and friendly that I shouldn't really have been surprised by the question. She thanked me and hurried off.

Ten minutes later she returned with her pale-faced and sickly-looking nine-year-old son, Dimitri. Ludmilla explained he had faulty kidneys. She would have loved to take Dima, as she called him, to a health spa in the hope it would help his condition, but that was well beyond her means. As it was she could barely afford the basic treatment he was receiving in the hospital. Dima was being allowed home for the weekend, which I could see his mum was delighted about, and she asked if I would like to join them for dinner at their home the following day. I told her I would be happy to take up the invitation.

On Saturday two schoolgirls from Ludmilla's English class came to Dr Victoria's house to guide me through dark streets (most of the streetlights were broken) to a tenement-style block of flats. Ludmilla answered the door and welcomed me in. Dima sat on the settee beside his little sister, both of them appearing to be happy and contented. It was evident from looking around that they were a poor family, especially having to pay Dima's medical costs.

We had a meal of potatoes and cabbage with tomatoes. Afterwards Ludmilla said Dima had a chess set and he would like to have a game with me. So we sat down on the couch, a cheap cardboard chess board with chipped and broken pieces positioned between us. As we played, this poorly wee boy kept handing me tomatoes to eat. It really touched my heart.

While I drank a cup of tea, Dima's sister climbed onto my knee with a Russian comic, talking excitedly in her own language. Ludmilla and I chatted about her son's condition and she said again how much she hoped a spell in a health spa would help him. What Dima really needed to save his life was treatment in a properly equipped hospital. Sadly Malin's hospital does not have the resources needed for the medical procedures Dima and so many other children like him require. Before I left I insisted Ludmilla accept a small sum of money to buy some toys for her kids. She didn't want to take it but I told her it would make me happy to know I could at least buy a toy for each of them.

It is moments like this, encounters with not just the children but their parents, seeing their everyday struggle and how they barely cope, that pushes me on to do anything I can to make life a little easier and their health issues a little more tolerable. I find it upsetting to think their need is so great.

When I first started going over I was shocked to see the doctors and nurses washing old bandages so they could re-use the dressings. That showed just how desperate their circumstances were. Each year I have tried to take as much medical supplies as possible, anything I could lay my hands on because I knew whatever it was it would likely be needed in the ward.

My holdalls have contained bandages, surgical instruments, operating gowns, disposable gloves, slippers for patients, disposable syringes, sutures, stethoscopes, blood pressure testers, diabetic testing kits, antiseptic gauze, swabs, baby clothes and, of course, money for the doctors to decide what else is most necessary to purchase.

With that money we have gone out and purchased many items over the years, including medicines, syringes, powdered milk, blood testing kits and dressings. I've also tried to improve the living and working conditions in the ward, so apart from the aforementioned beds and cots, some of the money has also gone towards tables, wall and floor cupboards, table lamps and telephones for the office because the old handsets were unreliable and often didn't work.

The kitchen didn't resemble anything befitting the name, so I purchased a fridge, microwave, electric kettles, electric rings, hot plates, pots and pans and food, so the kids could have better meals prepared. The toilets often had no toilet seats, so I've bought a few of those over the years, as well as other everyday items we take for granted in our own lives and which no hospital in the UK would be allowed to operate without – disinfectant, toilet rolls, soap, buckets, brushes, mops and soap powder.

Dr Victoria remarked that it would be nice to have a playroom for the children, because at that time there were no facilities for the sick kids to while away the long hours spent in the hospital. So we spent money decorating an empty room on the ward, putting a carpet down, painting the walls bright colours, covering the furniture with teddy bear covers, bringing in plastic plants and, of course, making sure there were plenty of toys to play with.

I purchased a computer with a printer and scanner, reams of paper, and had the internet connected, for which I pay the yearly fee. I also bought a radio, to help pass the time and provide some form of entertainment. There are no television sets beside every bed in this hospital.

By listing these products that have been slowly introduced to the children's ward over the last decade I am not trying to grandstand or show-off, rather I wish to demonstrate that when I state the doctors are working with nothing, I sincerely mean they have NOTHING.

Many of the items I've listed are not just basic hospital necessities but basic needs for everyday life, yet the authorities cannot provide even those minimum requirements.

What I am doing only touches the tip of the iceberg but I will continue trying to help until hopefully one day the Ukrainian government will finally take responsibility for its own forgotten people: the sick children who are the country's future.

If they live long enough.

Entering the Zone

The Zone. Alternatively known by many more macabre monikers – The Exclusion Zone, The Fourth Zone and The Zone of Alienation, to name a few I have heard over the years. Whichever title is used, each provokes images of a sparse, apocalyptic nightmare previously only viewed in a science fiction or germ warfare movie.

A 1972 novel written by Boris and Arkady Strugatsky titled Roadside Picnic, made into a film seven years later called Stalker, featured a forbidden zone depopulated of human life by an unexplained disaster. It was a scary foreshadowing, although the explanation for what brought about the real-life zone is all too clear.

Because if The Zone is an infected, solitary and twisted body, then its heart is the Chernobyl Nuclear Power Plant – its never-dying beat pulsing through the withered and collapsed veins of a once prosperous and growing civilisation.

Measuring fourteen hundred square miles covering northern Ukraine and southern Belarus, in 1986 it was home to 120,000 people living in new, prosperous towns and revitalised villages and hamlets. With one huge explosion the vast landscape is a wasteland, home now to only the steadfast few and an unnaturally flourishing wildlife sanctuary, and controlled by government agency, the Administration of the Alienation Zone.

Their presence is obvious in the high barbed-wire fences, radiation warning signs, gates, checkpoints and guards that outline the nineteen-mile perimeter around the power plant.

Welcome to The Zone.

This once thriving haven is now a lonely cemetery, where the abandoned buildings stand as decaying gravestones and the razed villages are buried within themselves.

I entered those cemetery gates on my first visit to Ukraine and saw scenes more heartbreaking and more frightening than the images broadcast on television and printed in the media could ever have prepared me for.

My journalist friend Anatoli was my guide and he has more than a professional interest in The Zone. To him, The Zone is home. Anatoli was born in Chernobyl village and moved to Chernobyl city a few years later. The power plant is named after the city, which is located just fourteen kilometres south of the nuclear site. Originally the power plant was proposed to be sited just twenty-five kilometres from Kiev. But it was felt this would be too close to an already heavily populated area and in retrospect it has proved to be a decision that saved thousands more lives.

Anatoli was at work as a university lecturer on the day of the explosion and only learned of the accident from a friend. Anatoli's sister, father and grandmother were in the town but he couldn't go to them or even have his questions answered.

The whole city was washed down afterwards, the top layers

of soil removed – as radiation clings to dirt and grass more than concrete – and the water piping moved above ground. The population of fourteen thousand was evacuated, including Anatoli and his family.

His grandmother, Maria, was like many of the elderly evacuees who could not settle in their appointed new home. She was eighty when the explosion happened and spent just one winter in her new home before returning to her former house, where she stayed until her death in 1994.

Maria was one of hundreds who disobeyed government orders to stay out of The Zone. Locally known as Samosely, literally translated to mean self-settlers, they could not find comfort in their new surroundings. Many had been evacuated to the big cities and longed for the countryside. They loved the land and their home and, being in the twilight of their lives, decided to spend their final days on familiar ground. Eventually the government arranged for food drop-offs but other people, who thought the Samosely would be infected, often shunned them. Lorries would bring the food in and dump it – they were treated like lepers.

I remember Anatoli telling me that his grandmother felt the aftermath of Chernobyl was worse than life during World War Two – and in Ukraine that is really saying something, as you will read in a later chapter. But he described the situation with the elderly people as being like that of an old tree that is removed and placed in new soil, it may stop growing. If it's a young tree, on the other hand, there is a better chance of it taking root and surviving. He still visits the graves of his grandmother and mother, who are buried in The Zone, and his old house, which I once went to with him.

So he is familiar with the people who work in The Zone, due

to both his professional work and his own background, and on this occasion he had organised it for a fundraising group of Belgians, who were hoping to provide care for some of the local children and donate clothes to the elderly settlers, to visit the area. Anatoli invited me to accompany him and he sorted out our documentation and drove us to The Zone, and through the guard checks, in his white van.

We were going to Pripyat, one of the most famous places within The Zone. The town was founded on February 4, 1970, built specifically to house power plant workers, although in those early days the construction workers were the ones who lived there.

It is situated on the right bank of the River Pripyat, hence the name, and located on land known locally as Polesie, vast woodlands and marshes stretching across Northern Ukraine and Belarus. With a railway, good road network and a port it was well served for transport for the predominantly young and bourgeoning population. Just before the accident there was a little under fifty thousand living in the town and, with an annual growth of around fifteen hundred, the population was expected to rise incrementally over the rest of the decade, especially with reactors five and six being erected at the power plant. These towers were abandoned after the disaster and the cranes remain in place to this day.

We passed by the so-called Bridge of Death at Pripyat, where many people are said to have gathered to see the colourful flames coming from reactor 4, little realising they were exposing themselves to huge doses of radiation, and moved on towards the town centre. The layout of Pripyat was based on something called the triangular principle, the idea of architect Nikolai

Ostozhenko, where the idea was to have wide, symmetrical streets with lots of space and a lack of traffic jams.

It would be crass to say the problem would never be an issue again but as our solitary vehicle drove along the dusty, eerily empty roads the feelings of isolation and loneliness increased. I watched the Geiger counter on the bus closely and every time it moved up, which was often, I could feel the uneasiness and butterflies in my stomach rise in correlation. It felt like we were the last people on earth and those images of old science fiction stories filled my mind again. It was extremely surreal.

I couldn't help but think of my own hometown, Cumbernauld. It, like Pripyat, was a new town built specifically as an overspill, in this instance for Glasgow. When it was founded in the late 1950s its architecture was lauded, although this is no longer the case, and for a long time its population was similar to that of Pripyat before the disaster. I tried to imagine the roads of Cumbernauld completely empty, trees growing out of the shopping mall or swimming pool, schools and houses deserted and ransacked. I felt a shiver go up the back of my spine and shook my head to clear the images. Such solitary conditions just did not seem possible, anywhere in the world, yet here we were.

We made our way into the centre of town, where the administrative buildings and recreational facilities such as the cinema, theatre, hotel and gymnasiums were all situated together. Many more leisure facilities and hotels had been due for completion by the end of the 1980s, before it all fell apart. I was interested to see the place but in no way could I say I was enjoying the experience.

It was here we were to meet Clarisa, a former employee of the nuclear plant who worked in its administrative office and also an ex-resident of Pripyat. She knew Anatoli and had agreed to meet with us and show the group her former home.

She once lived in an apartment in one of the many tower blocks that lined the streets. She looked no older than thirty-eight, which meant at the time of the accident she would be under twenty-five. A young woman just settling into adult life, having it all ripped away from her with little or no explanation as she was rushed from her home and evacuated along with the rest of the town's residents. Hearing the stories second or third-hand was painful enough, but the personal account was just tragic.

She led us to the sorry looking ravaged tower block that was once the source of so many happy memories for her family and many like them. Despite the guards and police, The Zone was the subject of pilfering and scavenging on a regular basis. Intruders often sneaked inside the barbed-wire fences and re-moved all sorts of polluted materials such as electronics, furniture, and even toilet seats. Most of this was done in Pripyat, where the residents had little notice or option but to leave their belongings behind in the days after the explosion. Graffiti was also a problem in the deserted town and there were many unsettling images painted on the walls of buildings all over Pripyat.

The hammer and sickle, Communist Party slogans, and other Soviet symbols and icons also remained on the front of tower blocks and buildings. It was as if we had driven through a portal to a moment in the past. The town is like the clock tower struck by lightning; its hands remain frozen and forever still at that point, while the world around it continues on.

Of course the lift was no longer operational in the tower block, so we made our way up the rubbish-strewn staircase and eventually reached the floor of her former home. She took us inside and spoke a little about her own situation, but it was obviously hard for her and she became quite upset. Through tears she described how happy and hopeful life had been prior to the accident.

Clarisa had lived in the flat with her son, who was due to celebrate his seventh birthday just a short time after the date of the explosion. We could see into the little boy's old bedroom, where there was a Mickey Mouse picture painted on the wall. By the time of our visit he would have been an adult himself, and I believe he lived with his grandparents in Kiev.

She pointed out the window and my eyes locked in on probably the most famous image, apart from the power plant itself, of the explosion's aftermath – the amusement park's big wheel. Clarisa said that for her son's birthday she had promised to take him on the new Ferris wheel, erected in the centre of the city behind the cultural centre. Of course, he never had the chance.

The funfair consisted of dodgems, swing boats, carousel and the big wheel. They were supposed to open on May 1st for May Day celebrations and it was long thought that the rides were never operational. But pictures posted on remembrance site pripyat.com in recent times show some startling pictures of children, young adults and parents queuing and riding the attractions. One theory put forward is that the park was opened early to keep residents entertained and distracted during the time between the explosion and evacuation. If true, that adds extra poignancy to the structure that should symbolise happiness and fun, but represents the polar opposite in Pripyat.

We left behind some vodka and gherkins, a traditional Ukrainian gift, to Clarisa for allowing us into her home and reliving those painful memories, and then we moved onto a nursery. We walked into a classroom and surveyed the scene – a dusty old piano in the corner, books opened on the desks, faded and smudged chalk on the blackboard. That eerie feeling, the end –of-the-world scenario, crept up on me once again.

We made our way back to the van none too soon, spotting through the trees an abandoned milk farm, and escaped the exclusion zone. Anatoli washed the vehicle down and cleaned it thoroughly and checked the wheels with a radiation counter on the way out, something he does every time he ventures into The Zone.

Over the proceeding years I visited The Zone on a few more occasions with Anatoli, but I had only ever seen the power plant from a distance. I had debated with myself as to whether I wished to go there. From the first time I visited Ukraine in 1999 with £100 and seen the hospital in Malin, I knew I had to return. Before the accident the children in the region were poor and didn't have much to their names, but the standard of living in the aftermath was something else entirely. Eventually I felt I had to see at close quarters that which had caused the suffering I witnessed every year.

Anatoli had contacts there and in November 2007 my friend arranged for us to go inside Chernobyl Nuclear Power Plant. We went through the initial exclusion zone checkpoint and again at the 10km zone.

As we approached the plant I realised just how big and vast it was. At the entrance our paperwork was examined and we were told to proceed to security. Here I was asked to hand over my passport, which was checked against the papers. I looked at Anatoli as the guard came back without my passport and my friend explained to me it would be returned on our way out.

Here I was, walking towards the place I had seen so many times in photographs and on television, described so intricately in documentaries and books. In one way it felt familiar to me because of how much research and interest I had in the accident, but on the flip side it felt an alien, scary place to me and I knew quite quickly it was somewhere I did not care to be.

I could see the concrete and steel sarcophagus that had been quickly built over reactor four in the months after the explosion, its precarious roof and beams bulging and threatening to expire as it held an estimated two hundred tons of nuclear fuel. What a sight.

I thought of the firemen and soldiers the government sent in immediately after the disaster. Did they have any idea what they were walking into? These men were sent into a burning, poisonous inferno with only a lead apron for protection, if they were lucky. Thousands of soldiers are said to have absorbed lifetime doses of radiation in seconds by making dashes onto the roof to shovel smoking graphite blown out of the reactor back into its core. An incredibly frightening thought. If a similar situation were to happen in Britain at Hunterton or Torness, God forbid, would our soldiers and firefighters be asked to do the same as their Ukrainian counterparts?

These brave men and others like them became known as the liquidators, the name given to those tasked by the USSR to conduct the clean-up operation. For six years after the 1986 explosion it is thought that up to one million people endangered their health attempting to remove the contaminated areas. Tens of thousands of these liquidators – an umbrella term for medical personnel, military, firefighters, construction workers, coal miners, reactor workers and Kiev's Civil Defence, to name a few – paid the ultimate price with their lives.

These liquidators razed many contaminated areas and buried the demolished contents under fresh soil and sand. This was the case with the famous Red Forest, a huge wood surrounding the power plant and now one of the most radioactive places in the world. Another of the famous landmarks from the Chernobyl aftermath, a radiation plume swept over the former Worm Wood Forest and killed the pine trees as the particles settled. The radiation discoloured the needles, turning them red, but most of the contamination was in the soil. Liquidators bulldozed the trees and covered them over with sand, before planting saplings on top. Over time some of these new trees have shown strange growth with twisted branches pointing downwards rather than to the sky.

There were a lot of people coming and going from the power plant as we walked inside. That surprised me. In December 2000 Chernobyl stopped generating electricity after an agreement was reached with European leaders. I imagined only a handful of scientists and nuclear engineers continuing to work at the plant from then on, carrying out radiation level checks and looking over the general condition of the buildings. Instead three thousand people still worked there at the time of my visit, just seven hundred less than when it was fully operational.

The employees work on a care and maintenance programme, since the damaged reactor, buildings, turbine hall, and reactors 1, 2 and 3, although no longer critical, must be continually assessed. The cooling pond water levels and radioactivity must also be monitored and recorded. So too have the Pripyat marshes for signs of leakage from reactor 4. A close watch is kept on that fragile sarcophagus, too.

They work four days on, three days off or fifteen days on, fifteen off, and are regularly tested for radiation. Most of them live in the city of Slavutych, built to replace Pripyat and located around forty-five kilometres from the ghost town.

I was amazed that so many people still worked at the plant and remarked such to Anatoli, who replied, "Well, they have to work somewhere".

A security guard led us along a corridor as a constant stream of people passed by us, coming and going from various rooms. We were taken to an office where a woman spoke to the guard, who then left, and she led us into another office. I was given some papers that I was asked to sign. Of course I had no idea what the documentation said, so Anatoli translated it for me and apparently it read that I was to agree I was entering at my own risk. The butterflies were fluttering again in my gut as I signed my name on the line. She gave each of us a white coat, hat and Wellington boots to wear while we were inside the plant.

She also asked us to put on a blue badge that tested for radiation. I recognised these from a job I had many years before in Wills Tobacco factory in Glasgow. I worked at the cigar accuracy machine, where a continuous cigar passes through whirring blades cutting it into appropriate lengths. Gamma radiation passed through the tobacco to take a reading to check whether it was densely or loosely packed. We had to wear a blue badge similar to the one I had just been handed, which was tested regularly for dangerous radiation levels.

An engineer then led us down another corridor to a secure

area entrance. He punched a series of digits into an old-fashioned keycode plate, but the set of doors failed to open. So he used an equally primitive-looking intercom next to the door to call a colleague on the other side and, after a long wait of around ten minutes, the doors finally opened. I found myself in another corridor with another door, which the engineer opened and indicated for us to go through.

I discovered I had entered one of Chernobyl's reactor rooms, just like I had seen on television so many times, just like the one along the corridor that was the scene of such horror twenty-one years previously. It was a weird feeling that I was experiencing, difficult to explain but certainly frightening.

There in front of me on the rear wall was the large circular layout of the reactor control rods, surrounded by a multitude of measuring instruments, displays and consoles. The floor space was taken over by the reactor's control panel with red emergency scram buttons, a floor-to-ceiling display giving a visual indication of how far the control rods were inserted. The reactor power levels appeared very outdated compared to those I had seen in Torness nuclear power station during a tour there years before. The ceiling was made up of white polystyrene tiles and the walls were a cream or light green colour. There was also one part of the wall that was wood panelled and had a digital clock display.

I could not believe I was standing in front of a control panel in Chernobyl and tried to imagine what it must have been like to be a reactor engineer in an identical room just one hundred metres away on that night in 1986. The frantic scenes as they tried to bring the situation under control. The desperation. The realisation of the catastrophic event unfolding before them. It was a nightmarish scenario and I could feel my eyes bulging as the thoughts raced through my head.

Anatoli introduced me to the controllers, technicians and engineers, and each one of them said how they wished they could still be producing power at the station. They simply did not understand why they had been stopped from doing so. I noted that none of the workers I had seen so far were wearing protective suits of any kind. I had two small Scottish and Ukrainian flags that I presented to them and they allowed me to take some pictures inside the room.

I asked if it would be possible to see inside the turbine hall or damaged parts of the plant, but I was told it was dangerous and would require me to be fully suited up. The suit I was currently wearing wasn't protective enough, I was informed, and in all honesty as I looked at it I couldn't help but agree. Anatoli said he would refuse to go into these areas and translate with me and, once the adrenaline had subdued, I was quite glad I had not gone any further.

From there we left the reactor and returned to Anatoli's car. Usually visitors have to travel around the base with an official but because they knew Anatoli they allowed us to go unaccompanied. It is only when driving round the plant on the surrounding roads that I gained a true understanding for just how big it is.

I saw again the abandoned construction sites of reactors 5 and 6, a host of cranes and other mechanised equipment discarded and rusting all around. Reactor 5 was almost finished and was due to be operational in late 1986 or early 1987, while reactor 6 was scheduled to begin producing energy in 1989, but all work was frozen and would never be returned to.

The hastily built sarcophagus over reactor 4 is another frightening sight, not only because of its shaky-looking appearance but knowing what is inside and what could happen if it were to escape its confines. Erected in six months and expected to have a life expectancy of twenty years, on my visit it was year twenty-one and even to this day the sarcophagus remains. The architectural work wasn't all that sound when it was built and cracks and splits have appeared over time. Some patch-up work has been carried out but it is not a good situation and there have been fears on more than one occasion that the original sarcophagus may not last much longer.

The concrete tomb is crumbling but for the time being it is somehow holding in place an estimated two hundred tons of nuclear fuel - some in the reactor core, some melted into the rooms underneath. Much of the structural support for the sarcophagus comes from the damaged remnants of the reactor, which had its one thousand ton roof blown off by the explosion. So it's not the strongest structure to hold up anything, far less something as important as the sarcophagus. However, maintenance over the years has kept it in place and hopefully it withstands the elements and time itself to remain safe until the new containment centre is ready.

A French company won the contract to make that replacement sarcophagus, known as the New Safe Confinement, which will be built on site and then slid into place. Once it covers the reactor the old sarcophagus will be dismantled safely, but the much-delayed project has already been suspended and postponed a number of times, extending the completion date by years to 2012.

One kilometre away, surrounded by security fencing and razor

wire, stands a large concrete building. Nearby are two huge silos, deep round holes going some distance into the ground. The
building is where the fuel from the reactors will be reprocessed.
Of course, the fuel from the exploding reactor is still down below under the sarcophagus. The silos will then store the reprocessed fuel, cooled by argon gas for the first one hundred years.

Anatoli told me about the sightings of giant catfish in the
cooling areas and water around the power plant site. I saw a
swish in one of cooling ponds as we passed by, but it was getting
dark so I couldn't see clearly. However Anatoli has seen them
and confirmed they are an extraordinary size.

We returned to the power plant office and handed in our personal radiation badges. I was not informed at the time if it had
recorded dangerous levels. We were then asked to stand on a
mechanical platform that was closed at both sides and had a bar
across the front. I was instructed to place the palms of my hands
on metal paddles on either side while my body was scanned and
checked for radioactive traces.

I knew I had only been there for a short time and thousands
of people spend their working day on the site, but I could feel my
heart racing as I waited for the bar in front of me to lift, a signal
that I was clean of radiation and free to go. Thankfully, after too
long a wait, it lifted and I stepped off. I was allowed to exchange
the white hat, coat and Wellingtons for my own clothes, as was
Anatoli, and had my passport returned. It was with a great sense
of personal relief that we left the power plant and returned to
his car, so we could make our way out of The Zone.

First though, we had to pass through the 10km check,
where the vehicle's wheels and our shoes were tested by a
dosimeter to make sure we would not be carrying abnormally

high radiation levels outside of The Zone. Once through that checkpoint I was happy to know I was moving away from the power plant. We passed through the outer security check and back into normality – if it's possible to call the standard of living and many people's hardships just outside the exclusion zone as normal.

I realised now that I was away from the foreboding power plant that I felt contaminated somehow. Whether it was all in the mind, knowing I had spent a few hours within the poisonous walls of the structure, I was not sure. I wouldn't feel clean until I was showered and had a change of clothes. The multitude of emotions I was experiencing were strange. Of course I knew what had caused the world's worst nuclear accident, but having just stood at the scene of the disaster, surveying it all, it was hard to comprehend. That outdated, monolithic structure had spread contamination across thousands of miles, causing untold suffering and so many needless deaths.

I know the world needs to produce enough energy to function, so maybe we can't live without power stations. While I would never claim to be an expert, if we must have these nuclear plants in our midst then much more money has to be poured into them to ensure they really are as safe as possible. Much better containment has to be put in place to be certain radiation can't escape, as a one thousand ton lid wasn't enough to keep it enclosed at reactor 4.

After nearly a decade of travelling to Ukraine, feeling shocked and helpless each time I stepped through the creaking doors of Malin Hospital's children's ward, I had finally visited the root of all the suffering.

I am unsure if I regret visiting the infamous Chernobyl

Nuclear Power Plant. But one thing I am certain of is that I will never go back. I would rather see the hope and innocence in the faces of those babies and kids, rather than feel the malignant and deadly spirit that hangs in the air over the epicentre of The Zone.

School Daze

By the time I made my trip to Ukraine in 2001, the world had become a very different place. The terrorist attack in New York on September 11 had shocked the planet and left everyone in an unshakeable grip of fear.

The loss of life in the World Trade Centre was truly devastating and the sense of grief and anger was still lingering. Whether these emotions would ever lift was hard to judge at that time, but even two months on from the attack it was plain to see that the way we lived our lives was forever changed.

In November, as I prepared for my latest trip to the Chernobyl area, I continued to watch the latest developments of the 9/11 aftermath on the news and listen to the theories of which country might next be targeted.

It was a rather apprehensive and uneasy time to be travelling to a foreign country. Certainly if it was difficult to fly with my medical supplies before it would be virtually impossible under the new flying regulations in the wake of 9/11. By now, though, I felt almost a duty to the hospital to make my annual visit. I knew the doctors had come to rely on whatever sparse supplies

I could gather from my sources in Scotland. Should any doubts have ever crossed my mind about travelling at this uncertain time all I had to do was think of the sick and orphaned children holed up in the bare ward and those uncertainties faded.

While I realised the hospital staff appreciated my small attempts at providing assistance in the form of supplies and whatever cash I could gather, I had no idea my trips were gaining wider recognition amongst the appreciative community. In one special day that I will never forget, I was made aware of just how thankful the Malin people were for my annual visits.

Anatoli usually accompanied me on the hospital trips to act as a translator but on this particular visit he told me he had to work, so couldn't accompany me. Instead he had contacted Dr Victoria and asked her if she would arrange for another translator.

When I arrived at the hospital, three teenage girls from the nearby Number One school were there to meet me. The trio – Anastasia, Tania and Yulia – were learning English and would act as translators during my visit. Later in the day, the girls asked if I would like to visit their school. I had never been in a Ukrainian school before. I'd developed an interest in the country's culture and way of life, so I was keen to see the education system at work.

However, later that morning the doctors also extended an invite. The following day at the same time as the proposed school visit, they were going on a wild boar hunt and thought I might like to accompany them. My daughter is an animal lover and I did not think she would be very impressed when she learned her dad had gone hunting, so I declined. Anyway, I'd already told the girls I would visit their school. I tried to imagine a group of

NHS doctors going on a hunt on their day off, but it seemed unlikely. I don't know, maybe it isn't.

The following morning I took the bus to Dr Victoria's house, a place I had become familiar with in recent years since I'd become friends with her and her family. Her son Anton, who was around twelve years old at the time, had offered to take me to the school, which was within walking distance of his home. On the way, we passed by his own school and he showed me round the grounds. It was an old, decrepit building and as we peered through a broken window into a woodwork room where Anton took classes, it was obvious the interior of the school was just as rundown.

We continued walking along the street until we came to a very large and drab concrete structure that was positioned on a lower level from the roadside. Anton pointed to a set of doors at the front of the building. "This is the girls' school", he told me, before adding, "I'll see you later." Then he was gone.

I walked down the steps towards the school and passed by a monument, which I understood to be a World War Two memorial. As I approached the entrance I wondered where my schoolgirl hosts were, since I was right on time. I pushed through the worn and scuffed glass and metal doors, stepping into a large reception area.

The girls were nowhere to be seen.

Instead, a rather stern looking woman whom I presumed to be the receptionist sat behind a wooden desk, the varnish long since faded. She wore old-fashioned clothing but her apparel seemed right within the walls of the jaded building.

I went over to her and attempted to explain in my broken Russian why I was there, but she just waved me on with her hand towards the corridor ahead. At the far end I could see a large crowd of pupils and teachers standing in rows. I thought I had stumbled into a school ceremony and immediately doubted whether I had come at the correct time. Maybe the girls had failed to tell the teachers of my visit.

I stood off to the side of the corridor and waited hopefully for someone, anyone, to come to my rescue. While I questioned what I was doing here, I became all too aware of the throng of girls and boys staring in my direction.

Just then I heard a shout, "Mr Gillies, Mr Gillies!" I looked up and saw Anastasia coming towards me. "This way," she said, leading me to the crowd.

What is going on, I thought, as I followed behind.

I noticed some of the children were wearing Ukrainian dress. These pupils stepped forward holding a circular loaf of crusty bread. The middle section of the loaf had been removed and filled with salt. One of the children broke off a piece of bread and handed it to me. I was instructed to dip it in the salt and eat it. I was still confused but did as instructed, while Anastasia explained that I was receiving a traditional Ukrainian welcome.

It was only then that I noticed the cameras and reporters from the local television station and newspapers. Anastasia told me they had come to cover the story of my visit. I couldn't believe what I was hearing. I had indeed walked into a school ceremony – but it was for me! I didn't know what to say.

While I tried to gather my thoughts together, I was asked to take a tour of the school. Although it has a lot of old and worn out facilities, the school's twelve hundred pupils hold it in high regard. They are proud of what it has, rather than lingering over what it lacks, and gaining a good education and qualifications are priorities for every pupil as they progress through their teenage years. They are sure to get just that at this school, which even has its own museum. It was dedicated to a former pupil called Nina Sosnina, a young local heroine of World War Two.

Experiencing losses of between seven million and thirteen million during the conflict, depending on which historian is believed, the Ukrainian people were at the mercy of two regimes that wanted to expunge them from the earth, those of Hitler and Stalin.

Regardless of the figures quoted, what is undisputable is that Ukraine suffered more losses than any other country in World War Two. Around twenty per cent of the fifty million total of war dead were Ukrainian. Yet its role in the war or the true extent of the devastation it endured – one in five Ukrainians died during the conflict – are little known in the world.

For a long time this was due to Soviet rule, but even when the Iron Curtain was pulled aside the fact that the country was left on its hands and knees during the war remained criminally ignored, a situation that remains true to this day.

However, the Ukrainian people remember only too well the suffering their kinsfolk endured, and as such there are thousands of war monuments throughout the country, just like the one outside Number One school's entrance.

Not only were the country's losses greater than any other nation, so too was Ukraine's material damage due to the 'scorched earth' policy of Stalin firstly, and then Hitler.

The 'scorched earth' policy was so called because any item of worth was ordered by Stalin to be destroyed so that the invading enemy could not use it. Whether this was railway cars, cattle or fuel, all property that could not be withdrawn before an invasion had to be destroyed and rendered useless. When the Germans began to retreat from Ukraine, nearly three years after they invaded in 1941, Hitler also instructed for such a policy left in their wake. The devastation suffered was as great if not greater than what had gone before. According to Soviet Ukraine the Germans razed and burned over twenty eight thousand villages and seven hundred and fourteen towns and cities, leaving ten million people without shelter.

Looking back to June 1941, when Hitler invaded Ukraine he faced little resistance from its people and quickly captured large territories. Quite the opposite. It is said that many of the residencies met the German Army with the traditional bread welcome I had just received when I entered the school. The Ukrainians were thankful because they thought they were being liberated from the oppressive Soviet regime enforced by Stalin. In reality though, Hitler regarded the Ukrainian people, like the Jews, as a sub-human race that must be wiped out.

According to an informative and detailed research paper by historian Andrew Gregorovich, Ukraine was to be the new living space, the Lebensraum, of the German nation. Therefore, Hitler planned by the end of the war to have the majority of the Ukrainian population wiped out with the remainder serving as slaves to the German people.

It is thought more than forty thousand Ukrainians were sent to Germany as slave labour every month at the height of the war. Professor Kondufor, a Ukrainian historian, said that more than two million Ukrainians were used for this purpose during the war. When compared to German deaths during World War

Two – over four million – the Ukrainian figure shows just how huge and catastrophic its losses were.

The Germans also starved residents of Ukrainian cities, prisoners of war in concentration camps, and those made homeless after the 'scorched earth' policy who subsequently perished. In addition, the death penalty was handed out to Ukrainians who helped or gave information to guerrillas; it was even enforced upon those who read anti-German leaflets and literature.

Which takes us to the story of Nina Sosnina.

Nina was leader of the Malin Underground resistance group despite only being a teenager. Born on November 30, 1923, her mother was a nurse and her father a doctor who practised medicine in Malin.

She was described as an excellent student, short and slim with big, sad brown eyes that gave her a dreamy look and golden braids stretching down to her waist. But she was soon to show she was more than just a capable school pupil. On July 22, 1941, one month after the beginning of the German-Soviet war, the army of occupation entered Malin.

Nina took the initiative and said what others had until then only thought: they must resist. After composing and distributing leaflets, she and her friends and acquaintances began meeting regularly at her home – along with father Ivan, mother Larissa and brother Valentin - to discuss various methods of resistance. Her charisma made her the natural leader of the group and she was looked to for guidance despite her age.

When Senior Lieutenant Pavel Andreyevich Taraskin escaped from a PoW camp and secured a job at Malin's radio station near the end of 1941, he was made leader of the Malin Underground District Party Committee. He immediately appointed Nina as secretary of the Underground District Komsomol Committee, in charge of the organisation for the entire district.

The family home became more or less a resistance headquarters and Dr Sosnin issued false health certificates to save members of the underground from being sent to Germany for hard labour.

Nina met one of her father's patients, a Slovak officer called Lieutenant Jan Antala, who informed her of the stationing of German units and rail transport. The Slovaks helped the partisans blow up a German locomotive and two loaded flatcars.

When Taraskin was executed on January 22, 1943 it was agreed that Nina should be the new leader. By spring the underground had gained strength in numbers and distributed leaflets, organised intelligence and carried out acts of sabotage.

Over the next several weeks Nina met a number of partisan leaders, who subsequently spoke very highly of the nineteen year-old. By now she was highly versed in the use of pistols, grenades and machine guns and she had sabotaged roads, blown up trains and attacked German garrisons. She was a force to be reckoned with.

But it was soon to come to an end.

On August 31, Nina and her father made their way to the house where a wounded machine gunner named Fedor Zinchenko was staying. He had been shot while fighting alongside Nina days earlier. Within an hour, truckloads of German soldiers and police surrounded the house. For four hours Nina resisted the Germans with machine gun fire and hand grenades. But eventually her ammunition expired and the enemy set alight the wooden house, killing Nina and her father.

Just at that moment the lights in the museum went out! We

all jumped. The timing of the power cut was quite unnerving and I admit to feeling a shiver go up my spine. The faded black and white photos all around me were plunged into darkness, but a torch fetched by one of the students soon provided a modicum of light while the schoolgirls told me the end of the tale. How strange.

The pairs' final resting place was a city park in Malin, where they were re-interred with full military honours in August 1944.

Twenty-one years later, Sosnina and Taraskin were granted the title of Hero of the Soviet Union while Dr Sosnin was given the Order of Patriotic War I Class. Her mother Larissa, who died a year later in 1966, was presented the Medal for Partisan of the Great Patriotic War. She was awarded posthumously the Medal for Bravery award.

In Malin, Teterev and Zhitomir, dedicated school museums were established. I stood in one of them. Nina's school across from the park where she is buried was named after her, as was its Young Pioneer Squad. A bust of Nina was placed in Teterev, and streets throughout the Kiev region – including Malin – were named after Nina Sosnina, teenage resistance fighter.

Once my eye-opening and emotive history lesson in the museum ended and the power was restored, I was taken back to the reception and asked to sign the visitors' book, while the lady in the old fashioned clothes looked on. By then it was lunchtime, so I was invited to eat in the cafeteria. Since the school falls inside what is known as Chernobyl Number Four Zone, under government legislation the pupils are entitled to free dinners. These meals consist mainly of just rice and pieces of bread, but I suppose it's better than nothing.

After we finished eating I was taken to the English class. On my way along the school's corridors I happened to brush against the wall and when I looked at my clothes I noticed there was a dusty white line on my trousers. I was told the walls were covered in a white dust, meaning if anyone were to lean against a wall then the dust would rub onto their clothes. I'm not sure if this was a deterrent to stop the schoolchildren from slouching against the walls or some sort of surface problem but I found myself patting down my clothes on one or two occasions.

As I went through the English studies door the pupils, already in the classroom, stood up and said in unison, "Good afternoon, Mr Gillies". I continued to be amazed at the reception I was receiving. The English teacher was Irena Krukovishka, one of my translators' mothers, and she asked me to take a seat at the front of the class. The headteacher also came into the room and listened as the pupils asked me questions in English. It was quite strange sitting there as the focal point and answering questions about myself, my family, my job and my life in Scotland, posed by people in another country.

I found it hard to believe they would be interested in my life or what I had to say, but then I noticed the media pack set up at the back and realised people maybe were keen to know more about me. It didn't make it any less surreal, though. It was their turn to question me now that I'd answered all the pupils' questions. The piece was shown on the television news later that evening. The local TV studios, incidentally, are located in a former guided missile factory, a very drab and dour looking building. A couple of years later I was introduced to the state governor. However, he already knew who I was because he remembered me from my appearance on the TV news.

Those newspaper articles also proved useful as an introductory tool on my later travels. If I'm having trouble being understood when trying to explain why I've come to Ukraine, I just show the person one of these articles because these explain my story better than my broken Russian ever could.

Before I left the school, the headteacher commented that she would love to have a real Scottish kilt to display. When I came home from Ukraine I told my mother the entire tale and she kindly gave me £50 to buy a kilt from an ex-hire shop. I took it to the school on my next trip and, after the physical education teacher tried it on to the delight of other teachers and pupils, the kilt was displayed in a glass cabinet in the school's corridor, where it remains to this day.

Perhaps it will act as a talking point for future pupils and as a reminder to the teachers of the day a shocked Scotsman was welcomed into their proud school with open arms and treated like royalty. As for me, no reminder is needed. That special day will never be forgotten for as long as I live.

The Orange Revolution

"The people who cast the votes decide nothing. The people who count the votes decide everything."

Those were the words of Joseph Stalin during his dictatorship over the Soviet Union from 1924 to 1953. By the end of the twentieth century it could be argued that this statement was still the case, at least in Ukraine. But by 2004, and with an election looming, the country's people decided they'd had enough of the lies, the corruption, the greed and the duplicity.

They demanded change. This time those counting the votes would not decide everything. The voters would. This was the Orange Revolution and during an extraordinary few days I found myself in the midst of a nation's brave uprising.

The foundation of the Orange Revolution was laid three years earlier when the true extent of the dirty deeds of the country's leader, President Leonid Kuchma, was revealed. Kuchma was the second president since Ukraine's independence in 1991, succeeding Leonid Kravchuk, who served nearly three years. Kuchma, a former Prime Minister, (in Ukraine, the Prime Minister is head of government and presides over the

Cabinet of Ministers in Kiev, but the President is the overall ruler of the country and represents Ukraine in international affairs as head of state) oversaw steady economic recovery following a time of decline and inflation during the tenure of his predecessor.

While the economy was back on its feet, pro-Russia Kuchma was throwing his weight around to push any potential danger onto its knees. He began imposing strict controls over the media, manipulated the political system and indulged in cronyism.

Kuchma, so far the only president to serve the maximum two terms in office, had by December 2000 seen his corrupt leadership plunge his standing in the popularity polls into single digits. Then a tape recording made by one of his bodyguards was publicised by a member of parliament and the lengths Kuchma was willing to go to keep a firm grip on his presidency was revealed.

In the tape, Kuchma could be heard recommending the abduction of an investigative journalist called Georgiy Gongadze, who had accused the president of corruption. Gongadze had gone missing in September 2000 and his headless body was discovered near Kiev nearly two months later. The revelation that their president was potentially involved in a murder inspired an uprising of sickened Ukrainian people to form an unprecedented movement known as Ukraine Without Kuchma (UWK) and take to the streets in protest. However, the non-violent group disintegrated when a Kiev rally in March 2001 saw a radical section of the group riot and attack the police. The authorities responded, causing dozens of protestors to suffer injury. The UWK quickly disbanded after this incident but it was a sign of bigger things to come and showed that the Ukrainian people were no longer prepared to simply accept what they were told to accept.

That was the muffled warning shot from an increasingly large portion of the nation, who continued to put up with Kuchma until the end of his term in 2004. The departing president nominated the then Prime Minister, Viktor Yanukovych, as his successor. Yanukovych was a safe choice and, with the backing and financial support of the government – at the taxpayers' expense – he was expected to win. Then 54 years old, the Eastern Ukrainian had an electrician and transport background before becoming vice-governor, governor and head of province council in Donetsk province. Kuchma made the pro-Russian the Prime Minister in 2002, despite serving years in prison for robbery in 1967 and rape in 1970.

Yanukovych's main opposition for the presidency was Viktor Yushchenko of Our Ukraine opposition bloc. Born in 1954 in the Sumy region of north-eastern Ukraine, he pursued a financial career after university, building himself up from village accountant to an economist working in local, regional and national banks on his way to becoming the first governor of Ukraine's national bank in 1994. His work in stabilising the currency and reducing inflation caught Kuchma's attention and he appointed Yushchenko as Prime Minister in 1999. Of course, his reform attempts and hardline anti-corruption programmes made him deeply unpopular within Kuchma's government and he was kicked out in 2001.

He quickly became leader of Our Ukraine, a reform-orientated coalition group that won the most parliamentary seats in 2002. The Ukrainian people looked at Yushchenko and saw an upstanding man who could finally bring change to their country.

He was by far the most popular politician as the election race gathered pace, despite the blatant propaganda-like material put out by the state-controlled media to make Yanukovych still look like a creditable contender.

In July, Yushchenko's Our Ukraine joined forces with the Yulia Tymoshenko Bloc to establish the Force Of The People. As part of their working agreement, if Yushchenko won the election he would nominate Tymoshenko for PM. At that point 44 years of age, Yulia was a striking, glamorous, wealthy and ambitious lady who exuded real presence. A convincing orator, she was the former president of United Energy Systems of Ukraine, a position that brought accusations of tax evasion and of selling large volumes of stolen gas against her.

Becoming one of the richest tycoons in the country, Yulia set her sights on politics and was elected to parliament in 1996, serving two years as deputy prime minister for fuel and energy. She became part of Yushchenko's government from 1999 to 2001, pushing through energy sector reforms. But after falling out with President Kuchma she found herself in prison for a month on corruption charges. Upon her release she vowed to unseat him. This campaign began in 2001 with her role as leader of the UWK movement, when her soon-to-be trademark impassioned and oftentimes combustible rhetoric was heard in all its glory for the first time. That same year she formed the Yulia Tymoshenko Bloc.

Viktor Yushchenko spoke out continually against corruption and expected Kuchma's government – which he called a criminal regime – to do anything to keep him from power. But even he couldn't have expected the events of September 5th. Following dinner with the director of the Ukrainian Security

Service, Yushchenko began to feel ill and, by the time he sought medical treatment in Austria five days later, the disfiguration and discolouration of his once elegant facial features were all too apparent. Rumours of poisoning were confirmed when it was announced that dioxin was responsible for his condition. While his health suffered and his physical appearance was forever altered, he valiantly carried on in the campaign trail.

While no doubt shocking it was, unfortunately, a classic example of Ukrainian dirty tricks. As I watched the drama unfold on television, I was not surprised at the turn of events. I had made enough trips to Ukraine and talked to so many residents that I knew such things were possible between political rivals in the country.

While all of this was unfolding I was counting down the weeks until I made my annual visit to Kiev and Malin. It had not really come into my thoughts when I booked the trip that I would be in the country while the elections were being held, because the initial round of elections was set for October 31st. I had simply picked a set of dates when I knew Anatoli would be around, so that he could help me out with everything and I could stay in his apartment.

In the run-up to that initial round of voting on Hallowe'en, the Orange coalition – so named due to the colour used in the campaign – worked with civic groups to organise voter education networks and an election monitoring system. This turned out to be a wise move. Yushchenko topped the list of twenty-five candidates with 39.87 per cent of the vote and Yanukovych was a narrow second with 39.32 per cent. Since no candidate had a fifty per cent majority, a run-off vote between the two top candidates was scheduled for November 21st.

As the stakes were raised in the election and the battle for supremacy raged, I began to worry about the possibility of large-scale civil disobedience, or worse, breaking out while I was there. I wondered what I would be faced with but I couldn't be dissuaded from going ahead with my visit. Despite what was going on politically, the hospital remained in urgent need of help. I reassured myself that Anatoli, with his large network of friends and journalist contacts, would ensure my trip was a success, despite whatever turmoil was taking place around us.

It was only when I arrived in Kiev on November 14th, that I truly realised this trip was going to be so much different from the ones that had gone before. There was a real buzz in the air, something I noticed almost the moment I stepped off the bus in the Ukrainian capital. As the days passed the electric atmosphere became more and more pronounced. The people were ready for change.

There were many complaints after the first election of voting irregularities in favour of Yanukovych, but since neither of the two leading candidates was close to having an outright majority and therefore the final outcome wouldn't have been affected, the complaints weren't actively pursued.

With this latest issue of irregularity in mind, and the long list of previous dubious elections, Anatoli and some of his journalist friends decided to carry out an investigation into suspected vote rigging. Piling into his minivan, which was being driven by his friend Yvgeni, Anatoli and I were joined by Tom Warner, an American reporter for the Financial Times who was based in Ukraine, and his fiance Iryna. Also in the group was another English-speaking journalist, Peter Dickenson, who has run such publications as *What's On* magazine in Kiev and *Lviv Today*. The final member of our party was an interesting and compassionate photojournalist named Ghary Sakrahan. I had first met Ghary several years before thanks to Anatoli and had enjoyed many nights in his company in Kiev, where he loved to chat over a vodka or two in Eric's Bar.

Ghary, who is well into his sixties, is originally from India but he left his homeland as a young man, driving his motorbike through Afghanistan, Iran, Iraq and Europe before settling in Holland. He has a Dutch passport and for several years he worked with a company from his adopted homeland that helped the Ukrainian street children. He supplied the kids with small cameras and told them to shoot whatever they wished, and then he developed the pictures and used them in exhibitions to raise funds for the children.

This minivan full of experienced journalists (and me!) travelled 500 kilometres east of Kiev to Ukraine's third largest city, Dnipropetrovsk. The reason we had driven there rather than observe proceedings in Kiev was because this city was seen as being more Russian than Ukrainian and was one of the areas where vote rigging was most suspected. Anatoli told me during the journey that in the first election buses were used to transport mobile voters, who were able to vote more than once. So called "dead voters", people who were recently deceased, had their former voting rights abused by fraudsters using their names. Our group hoped to uncover such fraud in person.

There were worries within the bus about being stopped by roadside security checks. As well as the usual routine stops where police check papers are in order, my fellow travellers pointed out additional roadside control points, presumably in place for the elections. My friends knew that should we be stopped we would likely be detained for further questioning, especially the foreigners in the group. But thankfully we reached Dnipropetrovsk without incident.

Upon arrival in the city we made our way to an apartment where we would spend the night. The flat belonged to an elderly lady, who had moved in with a nearby relative for the evening to allow us the use of her home. This is common practice in Ukraine, as it allows private individuals to earn some much-needed money.

The following morning was Election Day and we were up bright and early to visit polling stations within the city limits. We drove by many to observe the comings and goings, and visited several more. Tom Warner tried to interview two young women outside one of the stations. They told him they were too scared to speak, because if certain people discovered they had talked to a foreign reporter they might encounter problems.

The journalists had arranged to film inside the polling stations and take notes, and thanks to Anatoli, as an official observer I was afforded the same luxury. I wandered round the bustling halls and recorded the events on my camcorder, while the rest of the group carried on with their jobs. I noticed a number of people watching me as I filmed, a natural reaction regardless of the country, although they had more reason to worry about why they were being filmed, by whom and for what purpose than most. Several people spoke to me, no doubt asking what I was doing, but since I couldn't understand I simply smiled and replied that I was from Scotland!

Only once did I find myself in trouble. That was when I walked through a polling booth and out the other side to the transparent boxes where voters posted their papers, recording my movements. When I emerged from the booth an official approached me, talking loudly and angrily in Russian. He sounded upset. Anatoli arrived on the scene just in time and explained to me that this man was in charge of the polling station and even he was not allowed to pass through a booth during voting hours, far less film himself doing so. I apologised and Anatoli explained to the administrator that I was an official observer from Scotland. The gentleman told Anatoli that it was OK but he would require a copy of my passport. I handed it over and he took it away to make a note of my details. Afterwards I was allowed to carry on filming and I made sure not to overstep the boundaries again.

That night we went to a school where the ballot papers from one of the polling stations were to be counted. A number of tables were pushed together and around twenty people sat around them shoulder to shoulder. Each person collected a pile of ballot papers and sorted them into batches. They worked fast and when the counters were finished with a bundle it was passed to a woman standing at the end of the table. She would take the bundle and go through the papers one by one with great speed, announcing Yanukovych, Yanukovych, Yushchenko, and so on, almost chanting the names. A man stood beside her and oversaw what she was doing. Every so often he would say something as she was flicking through the papers and she would stop to look at it. Each time this happened, Yanukovych was the name she announced after a brief pause.

Occasionally a large amount of checked ballot papers were put in a large brown envelope and placed on a chair, and then removed when the bundle of filled envelopes piled up. There was no special seal put on the envelopes; this did not seem secure against tampering on the way to the supposedly protected building in the city centre, where only people of official standing were granted access to see the final results from all of the region's polling stations.

We stayed the night in the rented apartment and talked about the slackness, intimidation and abnormalities we had witnessed on Election Day. By the time we embarked on the journey back to Kiev the following morning we knew we were driving to a capital in the early throes of an uprising.

Unlike that first election in October, the blatant fraud of November 21st could not, and would not, be ignored.

Non-partisan exit poll results had given Yushchenko a marked lead prior to the run-off election; he garnered 52 per cent of the votes compared to Yanukovych's 43 per cent. Yet when the official results came in, Yanukovych won with 49.46 per cent of the count to Yushchenko's 46.61 per cent, meaning he had supposedly won by over 800,000 votes.

There was outrage.

The public knew they had been cheated.

This was the moment Yushchenko's Orange coalition had been expecting, preparing and educating for. At two am on November 22nd, while we had been catching up on some sleep in the Dnipropetrovsk apartment, Orange leaders broadcast an appeal to all citizens to gather in Kiev's Independence Square (Maidan Nezalezhnosti), known locally simply as Maidan.

The Ukrainian people acquiesced with the call.

It was time for a revolution.

By noon, nearly 100,000 demonstrators had gathered – mostly in Maidan but also in other cities. By the following day half a million had converged on the square, an incredible happening that left even the organisers surprised. The Ukrainian people had long ago had enough of the way their country was run and were now standing together for change. The world's media looked on, eager to see how the situation developed.

When I arrived back in the city I could hardly believe the scenes I witnessed. I was watching a bloodless rebellion firsthand and I felt that history was being written before me. I had never seen so many people gathered together in one place. It was something I would say again and again in the next 24 hours before I left for Glasgow, as the crowd continued to grow exponentially.

"Razom nas bahato! Nas ne podolaty!" ("Together we are many! We cannot be defeated!") Defiant chants filled the air and despite the cold, sleet and rain the protestors remained, with some estimations stating that one million people eventually took to the streets.

Members of Pora! (It's Time!), a youth organisation of about 10,000 members, were the first to erect tents in what would soon be dubbed Tent City. They organised and maintained order in Maidan – alcohol and drugs were banned from Tent City and trash was hauled away every day. Members of parliament, who could not be arrested under state law due to parliamentary immunity, erected a massive stage in the square on the first day of the revolution. Yushchenko and other Orange leaders addressed the throng from here and 24 hour TV coverage kept those Ukrainians who weren't on the streets informed of happenings.

I watched as hundreds of thousands of ordinary citizens blocked central Kiev. People from all walks of society, from Kiev and towns and villages near and far, descended upon the capital throughout the day. Families with young children, elderly people, students and lecturers, lawyers, homeless people, farmers, shop workers, labourers and housewives: they all were desperate for change so came to Kiev to do what they could to make it happen. Tent City began in the city's main street, the six-lane Khreshatyk Street, in those early hours and it would quickly become packed with protestors and their tents all the way up to the Maidan.

I was due to leave on the bus back home at ten am the next morning, so I decided to stay out in Kiev for the rest of the day and overnight, and go straight to the bus station from Maidan. This was a momentous occasion and I was determined to experience as much of it as I could. I also wanted to add my support to the gathering mass of humanity amidst the tents and makeshift camps.

I admired what the Ukrainian people were doing and truly hoped they would be successful. Nobody I knew wanted Yanukovych to win; he was Putin's man in Ukraine. If he did come to power, Anatoli's daughter vowed to leave the country. She was serious. I shared the view of my Ukrainian friends that when Kuchma was no longer President, the quality of life for the people could only improve. But if Yanukovych were his replacement, would there be a noticeable improvement? It was unlikely. The new president had to be Yushchenko, and hopefully the political changes he would instigate would result in more assistance and finance for the country's people and its hospitals, including Malin.

As darkness fell Ghary and I wandered around Tent City, my camcorder clutched in my freezing cold hands as I recorded the incredible scenes. We stopped and spoke with many of the protestors, who were in high spirits and resolute. I was surprised at how many could speak fluent English, a trend quite different to the areas outside of the capital.

A strong rumour was circulating the packed streets that at railway sidings east of Kiev a train full of Russian troops had arrived. They were waiting for the signal to come into the city and disperse the crowds. Was this true? What should we do? People were growing apprehensive as the story spread through the camp. I was concerned, too. If the troops stormed the square and were physical with protestors, the Maidan could soon be awash with red rather than orange.

"Maybe the militia will come," said one young woman we spoke with. "But this camp is peaceful. We don't even allow alcohol."

What we didn't know at the time was that Yushchenko and his staff had entered into dialogue with security force commanders and assured them the protest would be non-violent. As the days passed, both parties would eventually stand side-by-side in harmony.

I couldn't believe how cold it was. As the night wore on the temperatures continued to plummet until it was somewhere around minus10 or minus 15. My hands and feet were numb and I struggled to speak because my mouth was freezing up. My admiration for the Tent City residents continued to grow.

Some of the people we stopped to chat with offered us food. "No, you'll need it," we told these kind souls. "Good luck." We talked for a long time with a group of siblings. Natalie, a lawyer, was there with her sister, brother and friends. "What are you doing here?" they asked me upon hearing my accent.

I pulled out from my coat pocket one of the Ukrainian newspapers that featured an article about me. "You work for a newspaper?" one asked. When they read it they smiled and welcomed me to the country. "Are you proud to be here?"

I was proud. It felt great to be in Kiev during such a significant event in the country's history and I was glad to offer my support.

"We are here to fight," Natalie explained. "But it's a political fight. We have no normal life. Our fight is for the future of our children. I think the Ukrainian people support us and we will stay here until the end. However long it takes – five days, ten days, we will remain.

"I think we are strong and can fight for our democracy. We would rather die than be ruled by Russia through the hands of Yanukovych. Every Ukrainian wants to be a real European. This is not a question of geography, but of the mind."

Not everyone we encountered was friendly, of course. A tall, thin, wild looking man with staring eyes, pointed beard and long hair approached us as we walked by his party. He pointed at my camera and said something to me that I didn't understand.

"No, he is not state security," Ghary replied. "He is from Scotland and I am from Amsterdam."

At first the man didn't seem to believe us. Voices were raised between Ghary and this crazed individual. "You are an agent provocateur," Ghary told him. There was shouting and swearing but thankfully my friend stepped back before the situation turned really nasty.

"This guy is trying to cause trouble," a clearly irritated Ghary said, as we walked away from the confrontation. "You can't trust everyone here – there are double crossers, double agents," he fumed.

"Just try to keep calm and keep a low profile," I reasoned.

As the night progressed we met up with Anatoli and some other friends and moved closer to the stage in Maidan's centre, where live music from famous pop acts and speeches from supporters and associates of Yushchenko entertained the massive throng.

"How many do you think is here?" Anatoli asked me while we watched the action on the stage's big screens. We couldn't get anywhere near the front of the crowd.

"Easily half a million," I replied. "I've never seen a sea of humanity like this. It's amazing."

By now it was one big party atmosphere. Someone would shout "Yush-chen-ko! Yush-chen-ko!" and within moments tens of thousands were chanting the name in perfect unison. The enthusiasm of the crowds was rewarded when the man of the moment took to the stage to scenes of delirium and adulation. I felt fortunate to be there for this moment, and although I could not understand the words I felt I understood the sentiment his speech was conveying.

All too soon it was morning and I had to depart Tent City and be on my way to the bus station. I was disappointed to be leaving during this life-changing episode but I had to return to work just a few days later. Before I boarded the coach I ensured my camcorder tapes were hidden, just in case my camera was checked for content. The bus travelled through villages and towns where the streets were filled with people. Many were gathered round bonfires while others drove about in their cars, beeping their horn da-da-da in unison with the three-syllable yell of "Yush-chen-ko".

Once home I followed the latest developments from Ukraine

on the television news and made regular calls and emails to Anatoli.

On December 3rd, following the complimentary work of 300 lawyers who filed over a hundred court cases citing election irregularities, Ukraine's Supreme Court decided that the scale of the fraud made it impossible to establish results. A new run-off vote between Yushchenko and Yanukovych was ordered for December 26th.

That revote took place under intense scrutiny, nationally and internationally. Preliminary results released two days later showed Yushchenko had 51.99 per cent while Yanukovych managed 44.20 per cent. Yanukovych's team mounted a legal challenge but both the Supreme Court and the Central Election Commission dismissed it.

On January 19th, 2005 Yushchenko was officially named the election winner and he was inaugurated thirteen days later in Verkhovna Rada building, followed by the public inauguration at Maidan, appropriately, in front of hundreds of thousands of those supporters who were encamped there weeks before.

The Orange Revolution was officially over and officially a success. The Ukrainian people had united to force change in their homeland. The expectations on Yushchenko were huge. After the struggle to gain power, surely he couldn't fail now?

I had to see for myself, so I decided to make a quicker than usual return. I travelled to Kiev in March, just two months since Yushchenko officially gained power and four months since I stood in the hypothermic November night as Ukraine's citizens made a stand.

Life didn't appear to have changed at all, but then it had only been a matter of weeks since Yushchenko became president. Most people were willing to give him time and they remained hopeful of widespread change, but others were already expressing reservations about his leadership. In the period since winning the election he seemed most interested in building and strengthening his power base.

The election euphoria that swept people off their feet on my last visit had gone and was replaced by an apathy and outpouring of negative feelings. The people were disappointed in the realisation that very little had changed or was likely to change in the near future. After all the hope, the build-up, the demonstrations and the fight for a fair election, the people of Ukraine had been let down once again.

Unfortunately these early reactions and emotions were not unjustified. The great orange hope proved not to be the hue of a new dawn, but rather a hurtling, destructive fireball crashing towards the country and bringing the Ukrainian people back to reality with it.

Yushchenko went from hero to zero almost as quickly as his relationship with fiery and glamorous election partner Yulia Tymoshenko displayed signs of strain. Before the election and during the revolution they had put any personal and political differences aside for the greater good, but afterwards they could not make their egos and personalities work together to take Ukraine in a brighter direction after the warm glow of the Orange Revolution darkened.

Yushchenko sacked Tymoshenko as Prime Minister in September 2005 and, ironically, her successor was Victor Yanukovych. He was in place for sixteen months before the Orange camp pulled together to win the parliamentary elections, returning Tymoshenko as Prime Minister. But Yushchenko and Yulia continued to squabble, with the President accusing her of destroying the coalition because of her "thirst for power".

As a result, the decision-making was handicapped and the economic downturn had a devastating effect on Ukraine's steel industry. The banks collapsed. His weak leadership disappointed the Ukrainian people, who had been euphoric after the Orange Revolution. They lost faith in politics as a result of the comedown and also blamed economist and former bank leader Yushchenko for the financial crisis in the country, which forced it to accept billions of dollars in aid from the International Monetary Fund.

By the end of his first term in office, his popularity was so low – under five per cent – that he was unable to stand as a legitimate candidate at the polls. The only two creditable contenders as far as the public was concerned were Viktor Yanukovych and Yulia Tymoshenko. Despite the amazing efforts just five years before to keep him out of office, Yanukovych was elected president with 48.95 per cent of the vote compared to Yulia's 45.47 per cent. A Yanukovych supporter labelled the result "as the end of this orange nightmare" and the voting seemed to suggest this was the popular opinion. How quickly things change, but the shift in attitude was not altogether surprising.

Millions of Ukrainians believed Viktor Yushchenko wanted to help them live in a better country. That, unfortunately, was not the case. He let them down badly and showed he was nothing but a man full of his own self importance who was willing to trample all over former political friends to achieve his selfish wants.

If anything at all positive can be taken from the Orange

Revolution, at least the 2010 election was fair, accurate and democratic. It took a mass demonstration of people power to achieve that basic practice, but it worked.

And in Ukraine, that is big progress.

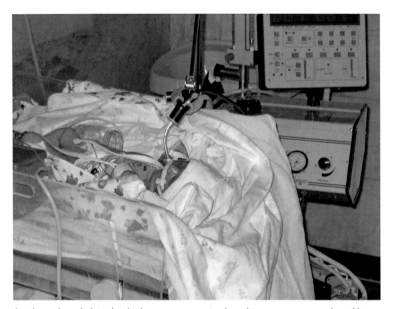

A sick newborn baby is hooked up to an expensive breathing apparatus, purchased by Jim thanks to donations from Sunday Post readers who responded generously to an article about Jim's fundraising efforts. Scores of baby's lives have been saved thanks to this machine.

Jim builds a desk for the ward's office.

A stony-faced Jim stands in front of the cause of it all, the Chernobyl Nuclear Power Plant reactor.

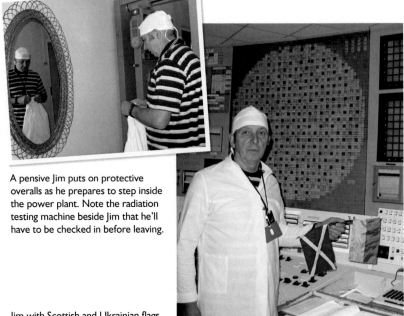

A pensive Jim puts on protective overalls as he prepares to step inside the power plant. Note the radiation testing machine beside Jim that he'll have to be checked in before leaving.

Jim with Scottish and Ukrainian flags in front of a reactor control panel.

Anatoli in the reactor.

Jim flanked by two reactor workers. Note the
military poses, a hangover from the Soviet days.

Jim in front of the huge concrete silos that will store the radioactive waste.

The two young women in the centre acted as translators for Jim on early trips to Malin.

Young students perform a traditional Ukrainian dance in a classroom during a school visit where Jim was treated like a celebrity.

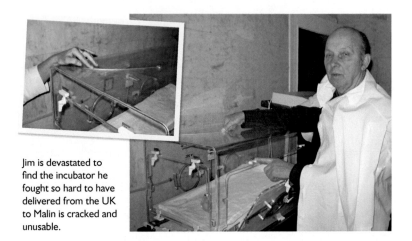

Jim is devastated to find the incubator he fought so hard to have delivered from the UK to Malin is cracked and unusable.

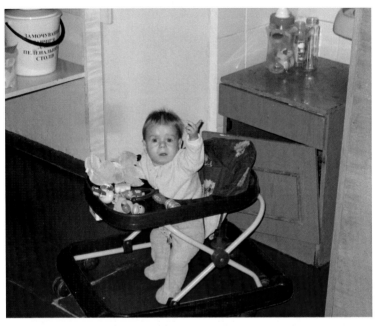

Jim's first sighting of 10-month-old Bohdan, the wee boy who could capture his heart.

Dr Victoria holds tiny Bohdan.

One year on, a dishevelled, dirty and upset Bohdan – wearing a dress – clutches the hand of his big sister, Alina.

More than a decade after receiving the letters that were to turn his life upside down, Jim finally meets Alexandr Lavrinenko, the man who wrote the passionate letters, in Ukraine. Unfortunately Alexandr can no longer speak English and so Jim fails to find out how Alexandr came to write to him in the first place.

Jim delves into the local cuisine. He's not always sure what it is he's eating, but he's willing to try anything once.

Jim samples some of the homemade vodka during a stay at a Ukrainian farmhouse.

A typical elderly Ukrainian lady, collecting water from her garden well.

Jim beside another well – a familiar sight in most gardens in rural Ukraine.

A sad toddler gazes out of a house in a rural village, with her grandmother looking on.

Jim didn't know what all the fuss was about when this well-dressed man walked into the bar. It turned out he was Slava Vakarchuk, one of the country's most famous musicians, and Slava had come to meet Jim after hearing about his fundraising efforts.

Vadyk Vakhrushev, Consul of Ukraine in Edinburgh, presents a scroll and medal to Jim at a special ceremony at Edinburgh's City Chambers in 2010 to recognise his fundraising efforts for Malin Hospital.

The Incubator

I looked at the dilapidated, archaic machine before me. It remained in the ward presumably because nobody had the heart to actually discard it. Here it remained, broken and useless, a sad symbol of everything that was wrong with the hospital.

"How can a maternity ward function without an incubator?" I asked incredulously.

The answer was as unpleasant as it was simple.

"It is difficult. Some babies die."

I vowed there and then to buy a replacement incubator for the hospital. How must a pregnant woman feel about coming here as she goes into labour? Does she know the life-saving equipment that might be required for her baby is broken and older than she is? That it is an obsolete and irreparable piece of apparatus from Czechoslovakia, a country that no longer exists?

It was 2004 and this was the first time I had seen the maternity ward. It was in a different area of the crumbling grey building from my usual stamping ground but the condition of its facilities was depressingly familiar. When I returned home I made it my mission to have a working incubator in the maternity unit by the time of my next visit.

Firstly I made inquiries to medical equipment suppliers but the price I was quoted for a new incubator, £4000, was far beyond my means. I would have to find a reconditioned or old model to send to Ukraine instead. Perhaps one of the major Glasgow hospitals would be able to provide me with an incubator they no longer needed or used. I contacted Yorkhill Sick Children's Hospital, the Victoria Infirmary and the Royal Infirmary. My links with the latter even afforded me a guided tour of its intensive care unit for babies. It wasn't just a world away from Malin's set-up but of another time. As the doctor showed me their state-of-the-art incubators, I wished Malin Hospital had just one working machine. She remarked how she couldn't imagine a maternity ward without incubators, yet that was the reality in a poverty-struck town in 21st Century Europe.

My pleas to one of these hospitals to donate an outdated incubator were falling on deaf ears. Staff in the wards gave me numbers to call for various administrative offices, health bodies and boards but it was all blind alleys and dead ends. Only when I called the NHS distribution centre in Larkhall did I finally find some direction. The stores manager told me that due to changes in the legal system any unwanted, surplus or obsolete medical equipment could not be disposed of to a private individual. The reason being that in the event of an accident involving said machinery, the health board that gave it away could be sued for damages. Now, registered disposal companies, such as GB Medical in Hampshire, England, collected all medical equipment.

I called and spoke to a gentleman called Tony Broadbent, one of the company directors, and explained my situation. He said they currently had two refurbished incubators in stock and invited me to have a look at their pictures on GB's website. The cheapest one was £500 and appeared to be in fine condition from its photo, so I decided to buy it using my credit card.

A short time later Tony called back. TNT International, the carrier company GB Medical used to transport goods, advised that it would cost £300 to take the incubator to Kiev. This was more than I expected but I knew it would have to be paid if the hospital was to have its lifesaver. I had received donations from my regular contributors, like the lady I'd met during a vigil and the retired miner from England, but this delivery charge would clear out my account for another year.

I arranged for TNT to pick up the incubator from GB Medical's warehouse and have it delivered to Anatoli's address in Kiev on November 6, the day after I was due to arrive in the city. The plan was that we would take it in a van from his house to the hospital, personally delivered. I received confirmation that the package was on its way. I was more excited than usual to be travelling to Malin because I knew just how important the incubator would be to the newborn babies of the area. I couldn't wait to see the faces of the doctors when we delivered it.

I arrived on schedule, but the incubator didn't. We waited the entire day but the TNT truck was nowhere to be seen. Anatoli called the company's premises in Kiev the next day to find out why we hadn't received a delivery. He engaged in a lengthy and quite heated discussion. I wondered what was going on. When he hung up he told me the Ukrainian Customs wanted the equivalent of £320 to release the incubator, the machine that was going to save the babies of the country's women. I was completely shocked and utterly disgusted. Anatoli wasn't surprised but I couldn't believe that bureaucracy was once again interfering in my attempts to help.

The following day Anatoli and I went to the TNT depot, a massive state-of-the-art complex that belied the archaic decision making of those inside. Despite a lengthy conversation with the impeccably uniformed customs officials, who had a control office within TNT's building, Anatoli failed to persuade them to reverse their decision. I felt awful as he told me the news. I stared at the officials, angry and disbelieving that they could be so harsh. Surely in the circumstances they could have waived the fee? I wouldn't have gone through with it to start with had I known about the charge, or I at least would have waited until I had enough money to pay for everything before pursuing it.

Anatoli suggested writing a letter of appeal to the customs officials and TNT hierarchy, which would explain my history with the hospital in the hope they would reconsider. My friend wrote the letters there and then, and read them back to me to ensure I was happy with the content before signing. We also decided to change the destination address, in case the situation dragged on beyond my stay, from Anatoli's home to the hospital. I hoped that wouldn't happen because the doctors had been made aware the incubator was on its way and were anxiously awaiting its arrival. The doctors also did their part by writing a letter asking for the equipment to be released for humanitarian purposes.

There was little else we could do but wait and hope. A few days passed without word, so Anatoli called the TNT office. I could tell by his expression that it wasn't good news. They would not change their mind. Policy was policy. To me, that translated as: no money, no mercy for the poor babies. I was devastated.

Anatoli said we must continue to try to change their minds by appealing to other sources for help. In his role as a journalist he had been told to cover a meeting of MPs at a university in Kiev a couple of days after we received the news. He knew there would be some influential people there and said if he could manage to speak to one of them about the situation then they might interject on our behalf. I went with him to the university, where we waited outside. President Yushchenko was making a speech at the event, titled "Our Ukraine" according to the banner above the entrance.

As the MPs and officials entered the building, Anatoli spotted the State Governor and said we should take the chance to approach him because he wasn't surrounded by his usual horde of security. My friend explained our problem. In response, the official told him to call his office and arrange a meeting with his deputy. I was delighted; surely the incubator would be released now.

Anatoli went inside to listen to Yushchenko's speech but I wasn't authorised to join him. Afterwards I watched as the President rushed past the crowd of people waiting outside the university building. Just before entering his luxury car, a tearful woman managed to make it through his heavy security team to speak to the country's leader. She was very upset and Yushchenko stopped to listen before jumping into the car and speeding away. As I watched him rush off from his people I couldn't help but think of those scenes in Independence Square one year earlier, when he was treated like a rock star by 100,000 Ukrainians believing he could provide much needed change for their country.

Yet here I was, fighting to have an incubator passed by customs officials because the government would not purchase the machine for the hospital itself.

The call was made to the governor's deputy and a meeting was organised for their offices in the City Hall in Zhitomir a couple of days later. Unfortunately Anatoli couldn't attend due to work commitments, so I went along with two doctors from the hospital. What was said at the meeting is a mystery to me since nobody could translate, but it lasted around an hour so I thought progress was being made. At the end of the meeting the governor's deputy handed me a letter. That night I let Anatoli read it and he explained that the governor's office was more or less saying they weren't getting involved and weren't willing to help. I just couldn't understand the mindset of all those involved in the matter.

My time was running out in Ukraine, so I decided I would have to bite the bullet and pay the customs charge from my own pocket. I couldn't afford it but I thought I might be able to raise the money through donations upon my return home, which would redress my outlay. I was so sickened by it all. The time spent calling, faxing and emailing just to find an incubator that I could afford would be all for nothing thanks to the Ukrainian officials if I didn't come up with the money. I indicated to Anatoli that I wanted to pay it, but after making another call to the customs officials we were told that I was too late; the change in paperwork was in the midst of being processed so I was no longer able to make the payment. I couldn't understand why this would matter. The letters we submitted had already been dismissed and the only other paperwork we presented was the change of address. Yet I wasn't too surprised, this was Ukrainian "orange tape" at its very worst. Perhaps I had upset a few people in power with my appeals and this was the punishment.

I returned home very disappointed but Anatoli promised he would continue to use his contacts to hopefully find a compromise and would keep me updated. An article was printed in the English-speaking Kiev Post newspaper about the situation, which kept the pressure on, and Anatoli persisted with contacting officials. I did what I could from home, calling the TNT depot in England from where the incubator was delivered. The only new information I could squeeze out of them was there might also be a storage charge for the amount of time it was being kept in the Kiev depot. Unbelievable.

In January, two months after it should have been delivered, I received an email from Anatoli. "It's terrible, Jim. The incubator is being returned to GB Medical," he wrote. The machine duly arrived back at the Hampshire business a few days later, complete with a £140 bill to be paid by me. As a donation, company director Tony Broadbent insisted on paying the charge.

After all the hard work, not to mention the money kindly donated that enabled me to buy and send the machine, it was now back at its starting place. I couldn't give up, but where did I go from here?

After a while I decided my best course of action would be to contact the Ukrainian Embassy in Edinburgh. Once I explained the situation they offered to help me obtain the relevant paperwork that would allow custom clearance and the incubator's free entry into the country. I had never considered approaching the consulate on the first attempt because I never envisioned there would be a problem. I thought GB Medical and TNT knew their business and I didn't consider that customs would charge for a lifesaving piece of equipment that would help their own folk. To my cost, I now knew better.

A number of months passed without word but eventually I heard from Edinburgh. All the documents allowing customs clearance was now in place, so I was free to resend the incubator and this time the hospital would receive it without a problem. I contacted GB Medical and gave Tony my good news. I paid £250 for TNT's delivery charge and organised the arrangements for my annual trip. Notification came that the incubator had left GB Medical's warehouse and was on its way. While travelling to Ukraine on the bus soon after, I wondered if I might see a newborn baby in the incubator while visiting the hospital. I was relieved the saga was finally at an end.

As usual, Anatoli went with me to the hospital to act as translator. I gave Dr Victoria the bag of medical supplies I had brought with me on the bus. She and the rest of the doctors at the children's ward were thankful, as always, but when I mentioned the incubator their expressions changed. What was wrong?

I was taken to the maternity unit and led into a small, bare room. In the corner was an old mop and bucket. This seemed a strange place to keep the machine. But then I turned round and saw an incubator pushed against the back wall. My incubator. The incubator I had fought so hard to have delivered to the hospital. Finally here it was.

And it was in pieces.

The catches were broken, the doors were completely bent out of shape and the thick plastic tank a baby would lie in had several large cracks. It was useless.

I couldn't believe what I was seeing. I was lost for words. I had a sick feeling in the pit of my stomach as the devastating sight sunk in. I looked at the sad faces of the doctors of the maternity unit and saw one with tears in her eyes. "It is a very bad thing to have happened," she said, via Anatoli.

I could only shake my head. The questions would come later.

Like how could the refurbished incubator be so badly damaged? Who was responsible? Who would pay for the damages?

I was completely shattered, absolutely devastated. Almost two years of planning and fighting all in vain and donated money wasted. Just to rub salt in the wounds the incubator was finally in place at the hospital, but rather than being a lifesaver it was only a constant, cruel reminder of the sorry situation. I was so angry, but more than that I was sad.

Anatoli suggested we try to have it fixed. If we could, the doctors would need to have the instruction manual translated so they could operate it. So we took the booklet away and Anatoli had it professionally translated, because it would have been too time consuming for him to tackle himself. We collected it a couple of days later, complete with a bill of £100 for the services.

I set to work on rectifying this horrible situation before I returned home. I was told Dr Valentina from the maternity unit had gone to the customs depot in Zhitomir, where it was moved after receiving clearance in Kiev, to sign for the incubator before it could be delivered. She had no idea of its condition at this point because it was wrapped up in packaging. Only when it was opened at the hospital was the damage visible.

Des Reid, the manager of O'Brien's, an Irish pub in Kiev that Anatoli and I frequented, was made aware of the situation and he told me his brother in Ireland wanted to pay for spare parts to be flown over to fix the machine. It was a lovely gesture, so

I called the manufacturers, Vickers, from Anatoli's flat. When I gave them the model number I was told it was really old, so much so that it was obsolete and no parts were available.

The reason I started this was because the hospital had an obsolete and broken incubator that couldn't be fixed. Two years later, I had delivered to the hospital an incubator that was obsolete and broken and couldn't be fixed. The situation was dismally ironic.

A bad situation was now terminal. There was nothing else I could do but attempt to seek compensation for the broken incubator in order to purchase another one. Firstly, though, I contacted GB Medical to ask if it had been intact and undamaged before TNT picked it up the second time. They said they didn't know, because the original packaging had been left on during the time the machine was back in their warehouse after its return. When I explained what had happened they said it was nothing to do with them, as TNT was the company that collected and transported the incubator on both occasions. I wasn't too happy with GB Medical as it was, because the incubator I had seen on their website looked much different to the one that now stood in Malin Hospital. On reflection I should probably have gone down to their warehouse to see it in person rather than just rely on the picture. The image on the website certainly didn't make it look so old that it was obsolete.

Anatoli called the Ukrainian TNT offices. However, he was informed that it was a matter for their English colleagues. So I phoned the relevant depot in England but they told me that since two weeks had passed between the incubator's arrival at the hospital and my complaint, any claim for compensation was nullified due to the time delay. I explained that the doctor who signed for it at the Zhitomir depot had no idea of the damage since the incubator was packaged, and once the hospital did notice that it was broken they felt it best to allow me to deal with the situation, as they knew I would be arriving soon. But TNT didn't want to know.

In a last ditch attempt I called other TNT depots throughout England and Scotland in the hope that I would find someone with enough compassion who would interject, but it was completely futile. I was more than £1000 down and all I had to show for it was a smashed-up incubator and a long phone bill.

I told my story to Clare Grant, a reporter for my local newspaper the Cumbernauld News, and she said she would try to help. After making several calls to TNT, Clare was eventually told that should I purchase another incubator, TNT would deliver it to Ukraine free of charge. This was not an admittance of responsibility for the damage, they added, but simply a goodwill gesture.

It was like scoring a last minute goal in a 5-1 defeat; it didn't really mean anything. For one thing I had no more money to buy another incubator. Secondly, I'd had my fingers burned with not only the obsolete model from GB Medical but also the delivery hassle thanks to TNT and customs. I had lost trust in buying a "refurbished" incubator and even if I hadn't, how could I be sure it would reach Malin in one piece? I would have to purchase a new incubator in Ukraine instead, but at this point I didn't have the required money.

I had to resign myself to giving up. I'd tried my best to deliver an incubator to the hospital but I failed. That was the bottom line. What I felt worst about was the donated money that had been wasted. Those kind people who gave their cash would have expected it to be spent on medical supplies for the children; instead it had been frittered away on a broken, obsolete machine and delivery costs and charges back and forth. Not only had I let the hospital down, I had also let down the donators.

Twelve months on in 2007, as I returned to Ukraine for my annual visit, I was still bristling with anger at what had transpired in the two previous years. So the news Anatoli told me upon my arrival was surprising, to say the least.

Representatives from the Ukrainian government had made contact with Malin Hospital, which was in itself remarkable, and informed staff that money was available to purchase an incubator. Anatoli had decided to wait and tell me the news face to face. It seemed our fight to have the machine released from customs the first time around and then the publicity from when it was broken had made those at the top sit up and take notice.

I was still annoyed at the £1000 that had been wasted and at first couldn't appreciate how huge and astounding this turn of events was, but it has since been pointed out to me and only now do I fully appreciate it.

Whether it was the letters of appeal we wrote to customs officials, the press coverage in Ukraine and Scotland, the intervention from the Ukrainian Embassy in Edinburgh, Anatoli speaking to so many of his influential contacts, the pleads from the hospital or a combination of all factors, I don't know.

Whatever it was, the Ukrainian Government did something they hadn't done in decades: they acknowledged the existence of Malin Hospital and paid for desperately needed medical equipment.

I was aware it would only be a one-off from the powers-that-be, forced into action as people needled and prodded from all angles. Once the incubator was purchased they would go back to ignoring the needs of the hospital and my missions would, sadly, continue to be indispensable to the doctors.

The damaged incubator remains in the hospital. At first it was a painful reminder of all I did to buy them an incubator before failing in the end. But from the bad comes the good and now there is a silver lining to the grey cloud that is the broken machine gathering dust in the empty storeroom.

It was the brief moment when we made the government take notice of the hard-working doctors and needy kids of Malin Hospital.

And that is probably the biggest miracle of all.

The Sad Story of Baby Bohdan

It was another cold November night in Malin and the fragile, flaking walls and gaping, warped windows of the hospital failed to keep the icy wind from blowing through the corridors. It was a Saturday evening and the children's ward was quiet, so I took a final stroll past the rooms while I waited for Dr Victoria to finish her shift.

We were to take a taxi back to her nearby tenement flat where she lived with her husband and son. When I visited the hospital Dr Victoria would kindly allow me to stay with her family, as it was easier than travelling back and forth from Anatoli's house in Kiev. Due to the lack of a shared language very little is said when we are together, we usually just smile and nod and try to get by with universal sign language, but I'm always grateful for the sofa bed in their living room at the conclusion of a long day in the hospital.

At the end of the corridor, in the final room of the ward, the door was slightly ajar. I heard a noise so I pushed the door open to look inside. And there he was. Looking to be around only a year old, the baby boy stood in a walker and stared up at me.

He had huge round eyes and such an innocent, happy face. A wooden bedside cabinet, its door hanging off the hinges, and a rusted cot, were behind him. If only he knew his circumstances I doubted he would look so happy and wide-eyed.

I don't know what it was about this little boy but he stood out to me and I could feel some sort of bond, so I was eager to find out what his story was and what had brought him to the hospital. Occasionally a child will stand out more than the others for one reason or another and I'll try to stay in touch or at least obtain updates as to how he or she is doing.

That was the case with Yana, a young girl I met in the hospital in 2004. She was three-and-a-half years old when I first saw her wandering around the ward, struggling with each slow and limbering step. She had curvature of the spine, amongst other medical problems, and had been abandoned in the hospital. Yana was a lovely girl, always quick to offer a smile to anyone who stopped to speak with her, and I wondered what the future held for this sick little orphan.

I found out the following year. In the twelve months since my last visit Yana had been deemed too old to continue living at the hospital, so she was sent to a state orphanage. It's a scenario that is repeated time and time again. There are many such units in Ukraine and the children living there desperately need help. I have only ever visited one orphanage in the country and it was in a poor condition, which I am led to believe is the case with most.

But now, as I stood in the doorway of the baby boy's room, I smiled as he waved his little hand at me. I felt bad for him. It was nine pm on a Saturday night and he was in this room all alone with no parent to look after him. I went to Dr Victoria's office and tried to ask about the boy. She told me his name was Bohdan Sobolevski but I knew I would have to wait until the next day, when Anatoli would be here, before I could learn more.

Thanks to Anatoli's translation I discovered that Bohdan Ruslanovych Sobolevski was born on January 15, 2007, making him ten months old when I met him. He came from a small village called Luki, about a one-hour drive from the hospital. He had been in the hospital for six months after his alcoholic mother abandoned him there. He weighed just a little over eleven pounds, not much more than some babies at birth. He also had several medical problems, many of which were caused by his mum's drinking and smoking while pregnant. These conditions included anaemia, statokinetic syndrome – which was a development delay – and xanthomatosis, a condition that causes fatty, yellowish firm deposits in the body. While these are harmless they often indicate other health issues such as diabetes. I felt so sad for this poor child and promised to do my best to help baby Bohdan.

But how? Well, Anatoli thought Luki might be one of the many villages heavily populated by Poles, so suggested I try requesting help for Bohdan from within the Polish community. Anatoli asked his brother, Vasili, to take me to the big Polish church in Kiev. Vasili is another interesting individual – he was training to be a cosmonaut and was halfway through his training when the USSR collapsed. He is also a former Russian fighter pilot and used to fly a Mach 31, known as the satellite buster because it flew right on the edge of the stratosphere. He couldn't speak English, though, so it made for another strange day out as we made our way round the city.

Unfortunately, at the time we went to the Polish church the

Archbishop had gone to Lviv for a seminar. He was not due to return for a couple of days, by which point I would be on my way home. Vasili also took me to the offices of Kateryna Yushchenko, the former Ukrainian president's wife and an American by birth. She had established a children's charity called Ukraine 3000 and Vasili and I hoped she might be able to offer some help or guidance. I was a little startled to see armed guards positioned outside her office block as we entered, but unfortunately she wasn't there that day.

I had failed to organise any assistance for Bohdan by the time I had to come home but I asked Anatoli to keep in touch with Dr Victoria for updates on his situation.

Before I left Malin, however, I sought permission to film Bohdan and the other kids in the ward with my camcorder. Upon my return I contacted Scottish TV, the regional ITV station, to tell them of Bohdan's story and to ask if they might be able to use any of my footage. A few weeks later they were in touch and asked to view my videotape to check if it was broadcast quality. I was delighted to hear STV was interested and excited that I might be able to tell a wider audience about Bohdan. Since I returned home I had been thinking of the best way forward and decided I should launch an adoption appeal for the wee blond-haired boy.

Now I just hoped my amateur camera skills were good enough for broadcast television. Thankfully they were and soon after I was invited onto the channel's live news and entertainment programme, The Five Thirty Show (since renamed and expanded to become The Hour), to talk about my trips to Malin and show some footage from my recent visit. I talked about Bohdan while his happy face was shown on screen, and explained how much I wanted to see him adopted and given the care and attention he deserved.

The segment was well received and both STV and myself received emails from viewers not only showing an interest in my Ukrainian jaunts, but also expressing a wish to adopt Bohdan.

I contacted Anatoli and told him of the feedback from the episode, and asked if he could find out what was involved in the process of a British resident adopting a Ukrainian child. Rather naively, I did not realise the difficulty in adopting a foreign youngster. Perhaps I had been blinded by the apparent ease of celebrities such as Madonna and Angelina Jolie adopting kids from overseas and thought it was a simple process. Ukrainian adoption law is tougher than most places though, as Elton John would later find out when he became attached to a baby from the country. He would need to find another way to become a parent.

On reflection I felt bad about saying on the show that I would love to find a new family for Bohdan when it was never going to be possible. I was embarrassed when I realised it could not be done and had to reply to these big-hearted people willing to open up their homes to this wee boy. Having seen him months earlier, abandoned by his mother like so many other children before, I tried my best to get him a better life. For that I make no apologies, but I just wish it had gone better.

As it was, I learned the state authorities were finalising documents to take Bohdan officially away from his mother and into a children's home. Anatoli was keeping in touch with the hospital and passing regular updates to me. Allegedly, when Bohdan's mum realised that she would lose her small state allowance for looking after him should he be removed from her care (although how she cared for him during his abandonment I cannot imagine) she returned to the hospital to reclaim her son. She couldn't dare imagine losing the allowance because that was her drinking money.

My appearance on The Five Thirty Show prompted STV's news team to consider doing a piece on my work at Malin Hospital, and in the weeks before my annual November visit in 2008 it was confirmed that reporter Debi Edward and cameraman Danny Livingston were to fly to Ukraine to film at the hospital while I was there. I was overjoyed because I knew it would help publicise the children's plight. I made my usual solo journey by bus and the STV crew were to fly in and join me for a few days midway through the trip.

I knew when Anatoli and I arrived at the hospital that Bohdan would not be there, but I was anxious to see him again and thought Dr Victoria would point me towards his mother's address. Surprisingly though, she said she didn't know where they lived. Other staff said the same thing. It all seemed quite strange. Anatoli told me he was quite sure the hospital knew of Bohdan's location but did not want me to go there. I couldn't understand why that would be and to this day I'm still none the wiser. Anatoli said to let him ask a few questions and hopefully he could find out where they stayed.

What Dr Victoria did tell me was about the plight of six siblings who had recently been abandoned. She showed me the front page of a local newspaper that had a picture of the kids, four boys and two girls, accompanied by the headline, "Mama, where are you? We need you, we love you. Mama, come home". The newspaper was three weeks old by this point and still their mother had not come forward. The kids varied in age from a baby to early teens. They had all been left at the hospital but the eldest five were moved into a holding institution until the courts decided where they would go. The chances of them remaining together were a million to one. The baby girl, Svetsana, which translates in English to Snowflake, remained in the hospital. Dr Victoria asked if we might spend some of the money I had brought on clothes for Snowflake, so we went on a shopping trip to pick up some essentials. When I returned the following year I enquired after the children and was told that while adoptive homes had been found for all of them, they had been split up. It was awful but all too familiar.

As for Bohdan, thankfully Dr Angela, another fabulous doctor in the ward who often accompanies Dr Victoria and I on the shopping trips, told Anatoli she would help us to visit Bohdan at his Luki home. A few hours later I was in the backseat of a taxi belonging to Anatoli's friend, Sergei, who had agreed to drive Anatoli and I to the village from Kiev.

After driving for some time through myriad streets with a noticeable lack of road signs, we stopped near a crossroads in a large village just before Luki. I saw a man walking along the street towards our vehicle. Just then Anatoli got out of the car and went over to speak to him. I assumed he was asking directions but to my surprise both men returned to our car and climbed inside.

"Jim, this is Dr Vadim, the local GP," Anatoli explained, as the man sat down beside me. "Dr Angela arranged for Dr Vadim, who knows the Sobolevski family well, to come with us. I have never met the family so we would be strangers arriving on her doorstep. Firstly though, we should go to the village shop to buy provisions for the family – but nothing that can be sold or traded for drink."

In the shop Vadim and Anatoli chose items like bread, cheese, rice, bananas, cartons of juice and potatoes. I wanted to make sure they had plenty in the house to eat and I had also brought with me from Scotland a bag of children's clothes to gift to the family.

From the shop we drove to an official looking building. Dr Vadim, who I learned was a French doctor involved in a charity initiative to take needy people to France for respite care, went inside. Anatoli explained it was the premises of the village council and Vadim was informing them of our presence, our reason for being there, and that the STV crew would be coming back with us in a couple of days to film. Correct protocol had to be observed, I knew, but I held my breath since bureaucracy seems to intrude in whatever I try to do in Ukraine. Thankfully when Dr Vadim returned he informed Anatoli that everything was fine and we continued on to our final destination, Bohdan's home.

Sergei followed Vadim's directions and we drove past houses and appeared to be heading out the other side of the village. As we reached the edge of a forest Vadim instructed Sergei to stop outside a single storey wooden house. It was surprisingly large although somewhat ramshackle, and was situated around thirty feet away from the next residence.

So this was it, finally we had reached Bohdan's home.

As we stepped out of the car into the bright sunshine and the surprisingly mild November day, I remarked how lucky we were to have this weather. Had it been snowing I doubted we would have reached our destination, such was the steep inclines and poor conditions of the roads on the way.

Anatoli and I picked up the bags of food and clothes and walked along the path across the unkempt garden. We followed Dr Vadim, ducking under the low doorframe of the house's entrance, and stepped into a hallway. Moving through a dusty and empty room, we went towards a connecting room. A man stood at its doorway, where he and Vadim exchanged a few words. He was called Nikolai and was a relative of Bohdan's mother, Natasha. On the other side of the door stood a young woman who was another relative, but she remained silent and just observed the proceedings.

We ducked through the low doorframe and there he was, little Bohdan. Sitting upright on a bed in this warm little living room, I recognised instantly the wee boy who had captured my heart a year earlier. I was so glad to see him but I couldn't help but feel sad when I saw the poor waif wearing mismatched dirty clothing, the upper half of which appeared to be an old dress.

His mother sat directly across from him on the same bed and she didn't seem to be in much of a better state than her toddler son. She really did appear to be a poor soul; twenty-eight years old going on fifty, her teeth were rotting, she wore mismatched socks and she was worryingly gaunt. It was quite obvious she didn't look after herself. I wondered what drove her to drink. Maybe it was the constant worry of health effects from Chernobyl or poverty that compelled her to go down the road of such self-destructive behaviour. Dr Vadim spoke to her and introduced Anatoli and I. He gently touched the kidney area of her back, making her cry softly. She was clearly a sick woman.

While they talked I became lost to their conversation and took in my surroundings. There was an open fire built into the wall, surrounded by pots and clothes as the fire blazed. The room was warm and I presumed this was where the family spent all of their time, despite the size of the remainder of the home. There were two old metal-framed beds, two chairs and a small cabinet in the living room. I realised I was looking at the worldly possessions of the Sobolevski family.

Also in the room was a young girl. Vadim introduced her as Alina, Bohdan's big sister, who looked to be around seven years old. I knew there were a further two children, but they lived in another town with their grandparents. The father or fathers of the children has never been mentioned in the time I have known Bohdan and I don't think he plays any part in his kids' lives.

We handed over the food we bought in the shop and the bag of clothes. It was smiles all round. I took a banana from the shopping bag, peeled back the skin and placed it in Bohdan's tiny hand. Despite being almost two years old, it appeared to be a new experience for him. His mother broke off a piece and ate it, and then she broke off another piece and gave it to her son. He seemed happy with his present.

From the clothes bag I pulled out a tin of shortbread that I'd brought from home. Anatoli, having been in Scotland many times, explained to them what they were eating.

Natasha motioned for me to pick Bohdan up and I gave him a wee cuddle in my cradled arms. I was so glad to see him and know that he was okay, or as well as I could have hoped for, anyway. Over those past twelve months I had often thought about him and the updates I received had only caused me more concern.

We stayed a little while longer before Dr Vadim explained to Bohdan's mother that Anatoli and I would be returning with a television crew in a couple of days' time, then we said our good-byes and left.

Two days later, Debi and Danny from STV accompanied us when we returned to Luki. Firstly we went to the shop to buy more food for the family. It struck me as we made the last part of the trip just how odd this all was; visiting a stranger with food so they could feed themselves and their kids in their own home. It was a similar scenario to having to buy beds for the hospital. Surely social care should be doing that? But of course I was all too aware by now that this was not how it worked in Ukraine. Even Debi in her brief time in the country had commented on the amount of 4x4s and Saabs she had seen in Kiev, a contrast to the abject poverty she witnessed in the days since. There is plenty of money and rich people in Ukraine, of that there is no doubt, but the wealth doesn't seem to spread to where it is most needed.

When we pulled up at the house Alina was there to meet us. She stood beside the car and as we came out with the shopping bags Anatoli suggested that I give her something to carry. I handed her a litre carton of orange juice, which she clutched ever so tightly in her small hands as she waited by the garden gate. The sight of her made me smile but I also felt a tinge of sadness. Anyone could see how much the gift meant to her by the way she gripped the carton, but it was all so little. Children at home wouldn't blink if they were given some orange juice, but here it was different. It only accentuated the feeling I had of wishing I could do more, because this was all so minute in the grand scale. It made me think of the other things they didn't have and desperately needed. I sighed as we went inside the decaying house.

There was Bohdan, looking happy as always. He was wearing a dirty jumper and looked a little grubby, but at least he didn't have a dress on like he wore on my last visit. Anatoli introduced Bohdan's mother to Debi and Danny. She seemed completely at ease with the camera equipment they brought inside. In fact, she did not really react at all to what was going on; she just sat there. I'm not certain how much she took in about any of it, if I'm honest.

Debi and Danny were great with Bohdan and Alina. Much like their visit to the hospital earlier in the trip, they showed genuine compassion and kindness for the children and it was lovely to watch. They weren't just doing their job, they genuinely cared and are lovely people, and I thank them very much. Before they left, Danny even left some money for Bohdan and his sister.

For some of the filming Danny suggested going outside since it was another bright day and it was fairly dull inside the house. Bohdan, dressed in a toddler's suit his mother had just put him in, was mesmerised by our car. He seemed to be particularly interested in the tyres, inquisitively running his tiny fingers over the grooves and ridges. As I watched him I thought of children I knew in Scotland of a similar age to Bohdan and wondered if he would have the same opportunities in life that they would. Simple, everyday activities like going to school and gaining an education, making friends and going on holidays.

Once Danny had filmed all the footage he needed, we went back inside the house and thanked Natasha. I asked Anatoli to tell her I would be back next year to visit once more. She asked me for my address so she could write a letter, but I didn't want her to have to spend money on postage, plus I would have needed someone to translate her words, so I told her I would just keep in touch via the hospital. I said a final goodbye to Bohdan and as I tussled his hair I hoped the next year would be good to him.

Twelve months later, my plans to visit Bohdan in Luki were thrown into chaos by the latest disruption to Ukrainian life. The world had been overcome in panic about a possible pandemic of swine flu, a potentially deadly illness. Unfortunately, Ukraine seemed to be held in the virus' grip more than any other European country.

To take with me on my 2009 trip I had old fleeces donated by the pupils from the local primary school where my wife worked, and £2000 cash. Around £1200 of that money was given to me by Christie Levein, the kind-hearted teenage daughter of the soon-to-be Scotland manager, Craig. Christie had watched the STV reports and felt compelled to help, so she did a sponsored skydive in Perthshire. Alongside her parents I watched Christie make the daredevil jump from thirty thousand feet and thankfully she landed back on ground without so much as a scratch.

It was hard not to be a little concerned by the constant warnings of swine flu. I had read online that the situation was worse in Ukraine than we were experiencing in Britain, but I had no idea just how bad it was until I received an email from Anatoli the day before I was due to travel. He warned me Ukraine had experienced more than four hundred deaths from what officials were describing as a mutated form of swine flu. I knew the situation must have been serious because he asked me if I would be able to purchase medicines for his family that would protect them. I contacted my local GP and chemist, but both informed me that the vaccination could not be purchased over the counter.

So I made my way to the airport the following day with trepidation. I had decided to fly on this occasion rather than risk travelling through several countries for three days within the confines of a bus, with germs constantly swirling around. Swine flu was constantly in the news and it was hard not to worry about it, although it did seem to be affecting younger people rather than those of pensionable age.

I flew to Gatwick without any problems for my connecting flight to Kiev, but on the plane from London I was shocked to find the cabin crew were all wearing face masks. It was the same at customs in Kiev and once I was in the city I found lots of people were going about their daily business with masks on. The country, once again, was gripped in fear.

Claims that pneumonic plague was sweeping Ukraine had followed the introduction of a quarantine, enforced after more than one-and-a-half million cases of flu. The pneumonic plague is a lung disease caused by the same bacterium as bubonic plague and is said to be the most virulent, capable of killing sufferers within twenty-four hours.

As usual, it was difficult to know the facts because the government doesn't communicate adequately with its people. The Ukrainians were frightened and there was a sense of panic because nobody knew what this disease was and medicine wasn't readily available. It wasn't until I was back in Scotland that I learned pneumonic plague is not found naturally in Ukraine and is a very uncommon disease, so rumours of such a pandemic were likely to be just that, rumours.

I had never considered not coming because of the swine flu but while I was in Ukraine it was a very uncomfortable and worrying time. The quarantine meant I was unable to travel to outlying villages, orphanages or hospitals. My planned trip to Luki to see Bohdan was cancelled. I was upset to think I wouldn't see him, but I was equally upset when I realised I couldn't visit the children's ward at Malin Hospital either.

But I spoke to Anatoli to ask if we would be able to seek special dispensation. Since the hospital staff knew us they said the restrictions could be lifted and we were able to visit. That was the first piece of good news. The second was that Dr Victoria had scheduled a check-up for Bohdan at the hospital during my visit, and he and his mother were to be driven down from Luki. I was so grateful to Dr Victoria for her thoughtfulness.

It was eerie walking through the hospital doors and seeing every passing member of staff, from receptionists and porters to nurses and doctors, wearing masks. A doctor told us of two people, a twenty-one-year-old man and a pregnant woman, who had died whose autopsies showed their lungs to be completely black and shrivelled.

I spent the day at the children's ward and gave out the school fleeces. Later on, Dr Victoria came to let me know Bohdan and his mum were here and she took me into a small room to see them. Little Bohdan was standing in the middle of the floor and he actually looked quite good. I don't think he recognised me, but then he was still only a few weeks short of his third birthday. I could see the change in him since my last visit – he had grown a lot and was looking well. That made me happy. He was even fairly well dressed.

Dr Victoria said Bohdan was getting better, but being aware of the extent of his health problems I don't know what that really means. I believe she didn't want to tell me too much, but he definitely looked to have improved.

His mum, on the other hand, just looked the same. She smiled and explained to her boy what was happening while I pulled his wee arms through the sleeves of one of the fleeces. She looked very ill. As I looked at the young woman's pale face I worried about what would happen to Bohdan and his sister if their mother passed away or became completely incapable of caring for her kids. Would their grandparents be able to look after them, as well as their two siblings? Would their father or another relative become their carer, or would they just be another number to add to the orphanage statistics?

My November 2010 trip was to provide some answers.

Anatoli and I arrived at the hospital in a car driven by one of his friends. A lift had been necessary due to the oversized, heavy suitcase I had with me, which was filled with children's fleeces and pullovers. I'd had to pay more money to the Polish driver at Buchanan Bus Station just to get my two cases on board, after he'd checked the weight of them and said they were far too hefty.

After giving out the clothes, Dr Victoria told Anatoli and I of the latest twist and dishevelment in the young life of Bohdan. He, along with Alina and another sister who had moved back to the family home since my last visit, had finally been removed from their mother's house and placed under state care.

I was told they were in a physiological rehabilitation centre in a village called Velykit Kobylin, which is around two hundred kilometres from Kiev and one hundred kilometres from the hospital in Malin. The nearest town to the remote village is Ovruch, a forty-minute drive. I'd never heard of the centre or the village before, but I was desperate to see poor Bohdan so Anatoli and Dr Victoria made enquiries with the centre about the possibility of me visiting.

A week later arrangements were finalised and we took a three-hour bus trip to Ovruch. The centre's director, a woman called Tatyana (Tanya for short), picked us up from there. On the way Anatoli and Tanya chatted and he passed some of the details onto me. The language barrier is never more frustrating than in situations such as this, when there is important and new developments that interest me but I have to rely on someone else to translate and explain. And quite often I'm only given a brief overview of the preceding conversation.

However, I did learn that the centre was based in an old school that had been shut due to a lack of numbers. It had been opened for around four or five years and could accommodate fifty-four children at any one time. It wasn't an orphanage in the strictest sense of the word, but a child could be adopted from the centre by prospective parents.

The level of facilities is better than that of Ukrainian state orphanages but poor by our standards. When I arrived at the old building I saw that the gym hall had broken exercise machines and a damaged pool table. This fundamental apparatus was probably what constituted the facility being called a physiological rehab centre.

I could quickly tell that Tanya and her staff were a genuine group of caring people with the children's best interests at heart. Of course that can only go so far without any money or proper resources.

We were led into the dining room where a meal was just about to be served. An urn of cold water sat in the centre of a table for the kids to drink from. The food is basic but compared to what most of the kids would have been eating were they at home it's good. A plate of fish, potatoes and cabbage was placed before me and as we started to eat, Bohdan was brought over.

I was so pleased to see him, but it was apparent that his health had deteriorated again in the twelve months since our last meeting. I noticed his eyes; those big eyes that had first made me stop in my tracks years earlier, and I saw something wasn't right. Through Anatoli I was told that Bohdan had cataracts. There was noticeable clouding in his right eye and at times his right pupil was in the corner of his eye while his left pupil was central. Apparently if the cataracts become worse he could lose his sight, so an operation is imperative.

While we were eating, Bohdan jumped up onto Tanya's knees and proceeded to eat her potatoes. The most basic of food yet even this was a real treat for him, believe it or not. Tanya said that since he arrived at the facility two months previously he had barely stopped eating and was beginning to put on weight. She also said his interaction with the other children and staff since he arrived had improved, because his social skills were near zero at first. So little attention had been paid to him in the past that he can barely speak and the words he can say are badly spoken, despite him being nearly four years old at the time of our visit.

I don't think he recognised me but Alina, who is now eight, smiled towards me and told Anatoli that she remembered me coming to their house. She said that she is happier at the centre than she was at home, because her mother drinks too much. Natasha is now in very poor health and drinks any kind of alcohol she can put her hands on. It's a terrible shame but what is even worse is the impact her illness has had on her young children. I was also introduced to an elder sister, ten-year-old Ruslana, whom I had never met before. They have another brother, but he is already in the state orphanage. Really, what chance do these kids have in life?

I fear that one of the reasons for Bohdan's poor health is because of the contaminated mushrooms he was fed by his mother. Mushrooms are eaten often and plentiful in Ukraine, mainly because they can be picked from the forest and therefore cost no money, an ideal scenario for someone in Natasha's position. But of course many of the wild mushrooms are contaminated thanks to the Chernobyl radiation leaking into the soil, rendering them poisonous. Eventually the public was warned by authorities not to eat them, but this advice was often ignored by people who are either cynical about the effects of radiation or by others who are so desperate that they will eat anything.

We spent several hours mingling with the kids at the centre. I watched the children playing together and talking with each other. Some appeared contented and happy, while others were visibly sad. The images of all those kids desperate for a break in life is one I won't forget.

In the gym hall a couple of the older boys asked me to play pool. As we played on the rickety old table the other children gathered round to watch, shouting words of who knows what and cheering when a ball was potted. My visit seemed to have generated some excitement among them, even those who had previously looked disheartened.

Later in the evening Anatoli and I were invited to go along with Tanya to the nearby home of her assistant, Natalia, for some traditional hospitality. We made our way down the dark, rough road by torchlight and in single file, passing by typical village houses with tin roofs. Natalia's home was also familiar in that carpet hangings decorated the walls and the toilet was outside. She served us various kinds of cut-up sausages and fish, accompanied by bread and pickles but I was still full from our earlier meal in the centre, so I only ate a little.

We later returned to the centre, where Anatoli and I spent the night in a couple of spare beds. The next morning we spent more time with the children and also met a nice couple who were in the process of adopting a wee boy from the group. They'd come to visit him and both parties looked pleased to see each other.

Just after we left the centre and were making our way back to Kiev on the bus, Anatoli said the most remarkable thing to me. He insinuated in a rather matter-of-factly manner that the centre's existence was down to me. His tone was such that he thought I was aware of this. But how could I have been?

"What?" I asked him, incredulously. "What do you mean it's thanks to me?"

"Well, remember when we chatted with the State Governor?"

I did. It was around five years previously and I had accompanied Anatoli as he went to cover a speech being made by politicians at a university. I had to wait outside, of course, since I had no media credentials but afterwards, when I met up again with Anatoli, he pointed out the state governor Pavlo Zhebrivsky. The official was standing alone on the university's steps and Anatoli remarked how unusual this was, because bodyguards usually flanked him. Anatoli said we couldn't miss this opportunity so he rushed over, with me a few steps behind, and he proceeded to tell the governor all about me and my work with the children in his region. I explained to the politican via Anatoli about the terrible conditions many of the children had to contend with and the lack of medical care at Malin's hospital, and that much more should be done to help those poor kids.

Apparently my remonstrations had touched a nerve because

Zhebrivsky made at least a small gesture, the setting up of the re-hab centre in the closed school. He must have acted quite quickly too, as the centre has been opened between four and five years.

I was completely stunned. Really, I couldn't believe it. I won-dered if Tanya or any of the other staff knew that I inadvertently had something to do with the establishment of the centre. To be fair to Anatoli, I think he had only recently found out about my connection to the place, perhaps when he was talking to the doctors in Malin while they organised our visit, but why he thought I would be aware of the situation I have no idea. I wish he'd told me before we had already left the centre.

The actions of the governor were only small, but it made me stop and think once again that maybe my visits were having a bigger impact than I realise. The resources at the rehab centre weren't great of course, but they were better than the alterna-tives. And if fifty-four kids at any one time are being looked after, fed and rehabilitated to some degree then that is a scenario that is much more pleasant to think of as I sit at home in Scotland, rather than the enduring images of Bohdan withering away in his mother's old house.

And as for Bohdan? Well, Anatoli and I decided it was time to once again take positive action with regards to the wee chap. He needs the cataracts operation sooner rather than later or blindness is certain.

Anatoli contacted me in the second week of 2011 to inform me that Tanya and Bohdan had made the three-hour bus jour-ney from the rehab centre to Kiev, where they stayed the night with Anatoli and his wife, Elena. The following day, my friend took Tanya and Bohdan to a medical facility in the city to be checked by a number of specialists, particularly an eye doctor.

Dr Elena Volymyrovna Akimenko examined Bohdan's eyes and carried out a number of tests. She confirmed he had no vision in his right eye, but would be able to restore his sight with an operation and also to repair the damage done by the needle.

"The needle?" I asked Anatoli. "What needle?"

Anatoli told me that when Bohdan was a baby, one of his sisters had pushed a sewing needle directly into his eye. His mother had obviously never bothered taking him to the doctor to have it looked at.

With Dr Elena confirming she would be willing to carry out the operation, Tanya and Bohdan returned to the centre to await the completion of some medical documents, which will then have to be looked over and signed off by Bohdan's local doctor.

While Bohdan was at the Kiev medical facility he was checked by a number of other specialists with regards to his lack of speech, psychological issues and a nervous disorder he seems to have developed. The likely reason for him being virtually unable to speak is quite straightforward; his mother barely spoke to him the whole time he was in her care. It's disgraceful.

Neither Dr Elena or any of the other doctors charged to examine Bohdan, possibly thanks to Anatoli using his contacts. But he informed me that the cost of the operation will be £500. At the time of going to press on this book I only have £55 in the fundraising bank account since I've only just recently returned from Ukraine. But if it comes down to Bohdan not having the operation if I do not put forward the money, then really, what choice do I have? I will simply have to come up with the money.

Once he has the operation, which will hopefully be a success, we have further plans to improve the life of little Bohdan, who turned four on January 26th, 2011.

You see, Anatoli informed me that the adoption rules in Ukraine have recently been relaxed somewhat, meaning that a Brit can now adopt a child from the country.

So at the end of December I went onto the national nightly news and explained the situation to the viewers. STV also showed footage I'd recorded of Bohdan on my most recent trip. I pleaded with anyone in Scotland who felt they might be in a position to offer a home to the young lad to make contact with me. I have to remain hopeful that something positive will come of this.

Regardless of what happens with the operation, at some point in 2011 Bohdan will be moved out of the rehab facility and into a state orphanage. He'll be split up from another two of his siblings and he might languish in the awful surroundings of the orphanage for years, waiting hopelessly for a foster parent to come forward.

I so desperately want him to have a decent life and proper upbringing, and in my opinion the best chances of that happening is if he is taken out of Ukraine.

I hope there is a positive upturn in the young life of my wee pal this year, because I feel this is make or break time for him.

But whatever happens, so long as I am fit to travel I will endeavour to visit, wherever he may be, Bohdan Sobolevski – the wee boy who captured my heart.

Another Life

When I first arrived in Ukraine I felt like an alien in a strange land. Everything seemed so different and the way of life was nothing like my own.

While I still don't understand many facets of the culture or some of the social and political aspects that are acceptable there, and probably never will, I have come to love the country. Ukraine holds a special place in my heart and it wouldn't be an overstatement to write that I feel at home there now. I'm comfortable and at ease, and it just feels right.

So much so that I find myself involved in activities I would never do back home in Cumbernauld. It's like I become a different person when I step onto that bus in Glasgow and by the time I arrive in the magnificent city of Kiev I am ready for whatever adventures come my way.

The following stories are just a few of the random events and observations from my visits to Kiev and Malin, which I feel demonstrate the kindness of its people but also show the distinctiveness in everyday life between home and my adopted land.

During my 2002 visit, Anatoli told me he must visit his

elderly aunt and uncle on their farm to help save their crops. An infestation of Colorado Beetle had been discovered on the potato plants and an insecticide would need to be sprayed on the crops to save them. He and his brother Vasili invited me along and for three days I experienced what it was like to live a rural life in Ukraine.

We drove to a small village approximately thirty miles south of Kiev called New Lubianka. Vladimir and Galina were in their seventies but continued to work the land, something they had done all of their lives, I believe. They obviously didn't have a lot of money but they were hardworking and proud people who would sell their produce at the local market to earn an income. When we arrived Galina, a small dumpy woman, was sitting outside taking potatoes from a pail and peeling them for dinner. She also had three dozen eggs beside her that she'd fetched from the hen house. Their home was basic and the toilet was outside, next to Vladimir's shed and the potato cellar.

Parked by the side of the house was a heavy metal cart containing a number of spades and hoes. I watched in amazement as Galina struggled to lift the long wooden handles and began pulling the cart. Their crops were around a mile from their home and were part of a former collective farm, the name given to agricultural land that had been under state control during Soviet times, where local people worked to produce as much as possible for the government. Following the collapse of Communism these collective farms were divided into plots for individual families to grow their crops.

As we walked along the road to the land, taking turns to pull the cart, I gave Galina a packet of Anadin I had in my jacket pocket to help the sore back she complained of. I wasn't surprised she was in pain, having to regularly pull that heavy cart up and down the dusty road.

When we reached their plot, which was around one hundred metres long and fifteen metres wide, we began distributing a pile of dung that was beside their patch into metal basins, so we could spread it on the field. There were many other people working nearby us, also spreading manure on their patches. I spotted one farmer who must have been financially better off, because he shovelled dung off the back of a horse and cart. Once we had spread it and sprayed the insecticide we returned to the house.

Galina prepared dinner and the five of us sat around the kitchen table for a meal consisting of produce grown on their land. There was a huge pile of fried eggs on a plate in the centre of the table. We also had potatoes, cabbage and black pudding.

After dinner I decided to go for a stroll through the village to walk off the heavy meal. It was like taking a step back in time. I passed by rows of old wooden and brick houses with corrugated asbestos roofs and outside toilets. Most homes had a well in their garden. Vladimir and Galina also had a water pipe in their garden for washing, but only water from the well could be used for consumption and cooking.

I saw a large wooden building up ahead, which I realised was the village shop as I came closer. Inside it was a poorly-stocked store, akin to the produce found in British shops in the 1950s. At the far end of the counter there were four or five women standing around a large block of butter, waiting to be served. The butter had two flat, ridged wooden paddles beside it; pats to collect and shape the butter. I remembered seeing butter and butter pats in a Glasgow grocer's shop when I was a young boy, but not since. Then I watched the shopkeeper totalling up a bill using an Abacus. It was quite remarkable seeing him use this method, although I later learned it wasn't an uncommon shop practice in Ukraine's rural areas.

On my return to the house, Vladimir proudly showed me his homemade vodka supply, which he kept in a large milk churn in the shed. He sold the alcohol to locals to earn some extra income but he was angry because a Latvian family had recently moved to the village and they were also making and selling vodka, which was affecting his sales.

We went back inside and Vladimir tried to turn on an ancient television set that was positioned on a table in the bedroom, so we could watch the evening news. The back was off the TV and a myriad of interweaving wires and cables were exposed. Despite tapping the insides with a piece of wood the television failed to function.

Instead, Anatoli and Vasili took me outside to a small sty where they kept a fattened-up pig that was being killed in the morning. This would provide a supply of food for the family over the next few days. As I patted the creature Anatoli asked me if I would like to watch it being despatched the following day, but I declined. I also met its successor, a small piglet that would suffer the same fate once plump enough.

After a good night's sleep later, I looked out the bedroom window to see the dead pig lying in the garden, killed by a stun gun to the head, while the family members stood around it with a propane blowtorch burning the animal's hair off. Later on I saw Galina pointing and lifting at various parts of the pig while a friend who knew how to butcher cut its limbs off. Once it was dissected, pieces were cooked and other parts stored for later. Nothing was discarded.

That evening I ate black pudding made from the pig's blood and also some of the meat. It was very tasty. I didn't feel bad eating the pig because I had personally seen that it was well fed and cared for during its life with plenty of living space, unlike factory-farmed pigs in Britain and elsewhere. I also felt this meat was sourced in a better manner than that I would usually consume at home, plastic packaged from a supermarket with no idea of its history.

It was an intriguing insight into the country's rural life, similar to thousands of other working-class people throughout Ukraine. The following year I experienced that way of life again, when Anatoli and I stayed for two nights on Vasili's farm. He lived in a small village fifteen miles east of Kiev called Vser, a Cossack name. He really was in the back of beyond; his premises were located just off a dirt road.

Vasili grows vegetables and also keeps a couple of cows on his land. While we were there he had a problem with the farm's water, so we had to collect supplies from a neighbour's well since Vasili didn't have one of his own. When we took a shower it needed to be late at night because the mains gas pressure was too low during the day due to villagers using their gas cookers or fires, meaning the shower water would have been cold.

In the evening we had a meal of potatoes and raw herring, and later I went across the road with Vasili to collect eggs from a neighbour who had a number of geese running around the garden. No mini market here!

I thoroughly enjoyed my forays to rural Ukraine, a part of the country regular visitors and tourists are unlikely to ever see or experience. I must admit I'm not sure if I could readily give up my creature comforts to live in this manner permanently. I certainly have a lot of admiration for the people who do live in such rural settings because everyday life seems to be tough, although maybe they couldn't imagine living any other way.

During a visit a few years ago there was a pollution problem with the main water supply to Kiev. Chemicals had made their way into the tap water. Residents were asked to go to the city wells (located in various spots in residential areas) to stock up on clean water, so when we were down to the last bottle of drinkable water at Anatoli's house, he and I took bags of empty bottles and containers to the nearest well to stock up.

It was a bright, sunny day but bitterly cold and the roads were iced over. We joined a long queue of pensioners, children, disabled people, workers and various others, who were waiting to collect water from the well. Eventually we made it to the front and replenished the bottles. Walking back to Anatoli's house we had to proceed carefully because of the slippery conditions, especially being laden down with the weight of the bags.

As we walked down a steep slope we saw a number of dogs running about in the distance. It's a common sight to see packs of stray dogs in the city suburbs but we watched them cautiously as they came closer. Suddenly a large black pregnant dog pulled away from the group and ran straight towards us. It brushed past me and as I turned to look round I nearly lost my footing. Suddenly I felt a sharp pain in my left calf. The dog had its massive jaw clamped on my leg. I tried to shake my foot but it wouldn't loosen its grip, so I swung one of the bags at the animal, as did Anatoli. Thankfully it let go and ran off.

Anatoli warned some nearby mothers out walking with their children about the dog. I was very worried about rabies, because feral dogs in Ukraine are known to carry the virus. Once back at Anatoli's house I rolled up my jeans and checked my leg. Although there were indentations from the dog's teeth thankfully the skin wasn't broken. It seemed the heavy denim had saved me but I didn't want to take any chances, so I decided to have a course of anti-rabies injections when I returned to Scotland. It's a precautionary measure I've taken prior to each visit ever since.

I'm glad I do, because I suffered another canine attack the following year. I was strolling through Kiev alone, having just been to a street market to admire paintings by some local artists. It was a beautiful part of the city and I walked down a steep, cobbled street towards the river, passing by a small theatre and a bronze statue of an academic looking gentleman sitting cross-legged on a bench. I stopped to take a picture and as I did so I heard sniffling and whimpering coming from beneath a parked car. I looked down and five adorable little beige-coloured puppies trotted out from under the vehicle towards a black and white collie lying on the pavement.

Just as I was about to take a photo of the cute procession of pups I heard snarling and a familiar sharp pain in my leg. I nearly dropped my camera as I jumped in shock, and when I looked down the collie was hanging onto my ankle by its teeth. I managed to free myself by spinning around and thrusting my leg, and the collie ran off. I had a couple of bite marks on my ankle this time but didn't feel so concerned, knowing I'd had the injections before travelling.

When I later processed my pictures I realised I had taken a

picture just at the moment of attack. Funnily enough I hadn't captured the line of five puppies, but instead had an image of the cloudy sky to remind me of the moment. I've now come to the conclusion it's best to stay well away from dogs while I'm in Ukraine, no matter how adorable they might appear to be.

I defy anyone to say Ukrainians aren't among the kindest people in the world, but sometimes their hospitality can be a little different from what we in Britain regard as normal.

"Would you like to taste Yivgeni's fish head soup?" Anatoli asked me, as we walked through Kiev city centre on a freezing cold day. Yivgeni was a former workmate of Anatoli and one of his best friends.

"Sounds good to me," I replied, trying to suppress a shiver.

"We'll go for some when we all meet later."

Anatoli and I were seeing Yivgeni, Indian photographer Ghary Sakrahan, his brother Vasili and Kosta, a dentist, that evening for some drinks.

We all met outside one of our usual haunts but instead of going in as planned we made our way to the metro. I thought we were going to Yivgeni's house to have some of his soup but instead we arrived at his lockup, one of at least one hundred of the metal structures located all in a row. We must be collecting his car and then going to his house, I thought, but instead we went inside the lockup. At the back of the structure were a settee, some chairs and a table.

"Take a seat," I was offered.

The place was painfully cold. I sat down as instructed, totally clueless about what was happening. Then I watched as Yivgeni bent down and picked up a large enamel bucket. A stone was positioned on top of the bucket lid. Yivgeni removed the stone and the lid, and then dipped his hand into the bucket and pulled out a dripping wet and enormous fish head, perhaps the biggest I'd ever seen.

"My God," I muttered. The men laughed and the fish head was plopped back into the bucket.

"Why do you keep that big stone on top of the bucket lid?" I asked.

"It's to keep the rats from getting to the fish head inside."

As a small butane stove was lit and the stock and pieces of the fish head were warmed up, I didn't see what else I could do but sit there, thaw out and wait for the big treat to be served. After a few vodkas I began to relax and worry less about the rats that would have scurried across the furniture we were about to eat from. I have to admit the hot soup was tasty and was finely complemented by the pieces of black bread that accompanied it.

This was Ukrainian culture and I loved it: vodka, beer and fish head soup, consumed in a perishing cold lockup on the outskirts of Kiev in winter. It was different for sure, but definitely not inhospitable or unfriendly.

Another example of that distinctive hospitality came when Anatoli took me to meet a couple who owned and operated a clothing factory in the capital. I believe he was seeing them for a newspaper article. It had been snowing heavily and the driving conditions were bad. When we arrived at the factory a path had been cleared leading up to the doorway; the piles of snow at either side were a metre high. The owner was there to greet us and he took us upstairs, where he and his wife had prepared dinner. I asked about washing my hands before we began eating and the lady indicated towards an enamel bucket in the corner. She took me over and I held out my hands as she used a mug to slosh cold water over them. No sink here. It was very brisk in the office and a small heater was produced to try to warm the room, unfortunately to no avail. However, they were a really kind couple and I appreciated their efforts towards me.

Anatoli has been a great friend. Without him I wouldn't have been able to do or experience any of the things I have in Ukraine. Of course, without him I wouldn't have even made it to the country. He often goes beyond the call of duty for his Scottish pal. On one visit I needed to change some euros into Ukrainian currency in a hurry, so we rushed down to the local bank. Despite it being ten minutes before it was due to shut, the bank teller wouldn't allow us through the door. Anatoli tried to speak with him but the man was adamant that the bank was now closed.

"Take your camera out," Anatoli instructed me. So I brought it from its case and held it in my hands, while he went back to the bank teller. I saw Anatoli pointing towards me and wondered what was going on.

A moment later my friend waved me over and we were shown inside the bank, where I exchanged my money. "What was that all about?" I asked Anatoli as we left.

"I told them you were from the BBC to do some filming and that he was making a bad impression of the Ukrainian people."

I just had to laugh and shake my head. Thanks Anatoli, for everything.

The funfair had come to Malin and I asked Dr Victoria if she thought her son Anton, at that time around eleven years old, would like to visit the fairground. He had never been to the shows before so he was excited when his mum told him. We went later that day but the few rides that were there were really old and shabby. It was a poor set up yet Anton loved it.

I looked at one of the rides, which consisted of a three metre long, rusty metal vertical beam with a seat at either end. The beam was rotated by an electric motor in the centre, and as two young boys sat on the seats and were twirled around, I observed that the chain connecting the motor to the beam didn't have a protective cover.

There were also dodgems, which Anton had a great time on despite their dilapidated condition. The cars were ancient and the overhead mesh they were connected to had broken sections all over, meaning that the cars often stopped and the attendant had to push them to another spot before contact could be made and the machines would restart.

As Anton whizzed around in a stop-start manner I wondered what he would make of EuroDisney, the gates of which I'd cycled to a number of years before. But then I also thought of the abandoned dodgems in Pripyat and realised that maybe Anton wasn't quite so unlucky after all.

I wanted to see some of the conditions the children who weren't in the hospital lived in, so Dr Victoria took me to a village around ten miles from Malin. I asked her to explain to the mothers in whichever houses we visited who I was and that the reason I wanted to film in their homes was to show the people back in Scotland. I hoped the images might inspire donations.

We went to one house where the woman had ten children. She was obviously very poor and the house was cold, despite the fire burning in the built-in stove, where a large pot stuffed full of potatoes and cabbage sat. Above the stove a piece of string was stretched across and a selection of grubby-looking children's clothes were draped over it. There was a large bed in the corner with clothes scattered around it and a very old babushka sat on a wooden box. Behind her was an open doorway into another room containing a bed but I could see a lot of plaster from the wall lying on the floor. Apparently this room was too damp to use, so much so it would affect the kids' health.

Some of her children were at school at the time of our visit, while others lived with relatives. But one of her sons was there at the time. He was around nine years old and stood shivering, so I took off the fleece I was wearing and put it over his shoulders, saying "padarak" (present). The wee chap was so happy and gave me a wonderfully big smile in response.

The next house we visited was in a similar condition and I left my scarf, gloves and hat with the occupants. In a way I was thankful that I was only in two houses because I had given away all of my warm clothes and had nothing left to give, apart from the shirt, trousers and shoes that I wore.

It's not all work, of course, Kiev has a vibrant social scene and I have spent many a fun and interesting night in Eric's Bierstube in the city centre. Eric Aigner is a German man who was once a well-known entrepreneur in Kiev's bar and club network. He had many connections with celebrities, as the numerous pictures behind the bar of him arm-in-arm with a famous face demonstrated. In my most recent trips, however, Eric had gone and the bar was under new management. I wasn't able to ascertain exactly why Eric had moved on, although I believe he now lives in Odessa. The Bierstube continues to be affectionately known as Eric's in his honour.

There is a small bar in the upstairs terrace but the real action takes place in the basement, where the atmosphere is usually buzzing in the evenings. It's a popular venue for ex-pats and Ukrainian businessmen and most of the group that I socialise with here can speak English. It wasn't unusual to find us gathered round a table drinking vodka and gabbing away until two am.

On one occasion Peter Dickinson, the English journalist who at the time edited What's On magazine in Kiev, brought someone in to Eric's to meet me. As Peter and this young man walked into the basement I went over to be introduced, but as I did so I realised all eyes from the bar's patrons were on us. Before I knew it people had swarmed to this man and, by close association, me.

Young men and women alike were clamouring at him, asking for autographs and posing for pictures. When the interest died down we stood at the bar and chatted, and I discovered that Svyatoslav (Slava) Vakarchuk was one of the most famous, and brightest, celebrities in Ukraine. Born in 1975, Slava is the son of a professor of physics who later became a high-ranking politician. Slava himself has a degree in theoretical physics but he decided to go down the entertainment route and became a successful singer with the band, Okean Elzy. They have released several best-selling albums, played all around Europe including London, and Slava has even won the top prize in the Ukrainian version of Who Wants To Be A Millionaire.

We talked at the bar for quite some time and he seemed interested in my ongoing work in Malin. Since that night Slava has gone onto become an even bigger star. He was very supportive of the Orange Revolution and followed in his father's footsteps by becoming involved in politics. He became a member of Yanukovych's parliamentary committee for freedom of speech questions, but later renounced his seat due to the dire political situation. He continues to write and record music, releasing a solo album in addition to his work with Okean Elzy.

Another one of my favourite bars in Kiev is O'Brien's, an Irish pub that was one of the first Western-style drinking establishments to set up in the city. It was run by a genuine Irishman in Desmond Reid and was popular among ex-pats as well as local business people. It serves Guinness and good bar food, and shows football on the big screens and often has live music. I became good friends with Desmond, but when I went into the bar during my 2008 visit I was told there had been a problem and he no longer worked at O'Brien's, which was disappointing.

Not all trips to Kiev's bars have been so enjoyable, though. Anatoli took me to a pub one night that I'd never visited before. It was very crowded but I managed to find a free stool by the bar. Just after I sat down, the man beside me started shoving and pushing me. He was shouting as well and seemed really angry.

"What's your problem?" I snapped, trying to keep my balance. I was quite taken aback by his uncalled for aggression.

Anatoli interjected and they began shouting back and forth, while I sat in the middle bemused by it all. I understood my friend telling this guy that I was from Scotland. What was going on? Anatoli turned to me and said, "This man is Ukrainian and he dislikes Russians. He thinks you are Russian and doesn't believe me when I tell him you're Scottish. Could you please tell him in English you're from Scotland."

I turned to my aggressor. "My name's Jim and I live in Scotland."

I waited to see what would happen next.

The man, who I presumed couldn't speak English, seemed satisfied with my foreign statement and he shook my hand before moving further down the bar. I definitely needed a drink after this strange little incident.

But as I took a large sip of my vodka, I realised the excitement wasn't over just yet. Two military men marched into the bar and the crowd of people parted as they approached us. They spoke to the barmaid, who motioned towards me, and then they came over. Anatoli spoke to them. He explained to me that they needed to see my passport. I had learned early on in my Ukrainian travels to always keep my personal documents on me, so I brought it from my jacket pocket and they examined it. What is going on here, I thought. My heart was racing.

They seemed satisfied because they thanked me and returned my passport. I breathed a sigh of relief as they walked away, but then I realised the military men weren't leaving the bar just quite yet. The pair marched over to the Russian-hater and spoke to him. They pulled him to his feet and guided him out of the premises. This seemed a little over the top but it was an eye-opening indication of not just the bad feeling between the natives of the neighbouring countries, but also the omnipotent rule and command of the authorities in Ukraine.

"Next time we'll just go to Eric's," I told Anatoli, as I drained my glass.

After more than a decade visiting Kiev and Malin, one might imagine that I would be quite au fait with navigating and travelling around by now. When I'm with someone that is generally the case, but on the rare occasions I make a solo journey I can sometimes lose my way.

For example, during my 2007 visit I became quite disorientated during a trip from Kiev to Malin. Two days earlier I had travelled by metro and mini bus with Anatoli, as we had done many times before, and we arrived at our destination without a problem. Now I was returning alone to drop off a holdall of clothes at the hospital.

I purchased a metro ticket and got on the train, but after two stops I realised I was going in the wrong direction. So I disembarked at the next station, waited for one that was travelling in the opposite direction and went back to my starting point, where I checked the list of stations and lines once again. This time I counted the number of stops that would take me to the station close by the minibus terminus. It was sardine time on the metro, so when I got on the train I made sure to stand near to the door.

This time I arrived at the correct station. I was sure I would still be at the hospital for the arranged time of one pm. But as I wandered through the vast underground concourse, passing by the rushing commuters and the stallholders selling all types of goods, I realised I had no idea how to find my way to the minibus stop. I went up one set of stairs but the terminus was nowhere to be seen. So I went back down the steps and up another set further along the tunnel, but still no luck. I tried asking a few people but either they didn't understand me or I them.

I tried another exit and emerged into a market area with lots of stalls and shops located beside a busy road. I attempted asking at a few of the stores for directions but again communication was proving impossible. I made my way over some rough ground behind a shoe stall and came to a railway line. Beyond the railings of the train tracks I could see a bus station, my bus station. Thank goodness.

I couldn't access it from here though, so I had to go back down into the labyrinthine underground. Slowly I made my way along a route that I believed would take me to the station. When I reached the top of the steps I was relieved to see I'd finally come out at the correct exit. I hurried across the road to the parked minibuses, aware I was already running late. But there was more trouble. I couldn't find the Malin bus.

I walked about the terminus for fifteen minutes, looking for my bus and trying to ask queuing passengers if they knew where I could find it. As usual though, my accent wasn't understood. Finally I stumbled across the correct bus but when I hurried forward with my large holdall the driver told me there was no room for my luggage. I would have to wait for the next coach. At least I knew I was now in the correct area, even if I did have to wait another half hour.

I had just boarded when my mobile rang. It was the hospital.

"Where are you, Jim?" I understood Dr Victoria say, but my language wasn't good enough to form a reply.

I turned round to the woman sitting behind me and said to her in Russian, "Please talk to my doctor friend," and handed her the phone. She looked puzzled but took the mobile from my hand and put it to her ear.

A smile broke across her face as Dr Victoria spoke to her. When she returned the phone to me I said to Victoria, "Understand?"

"Yes," she replied and I hung up, relieved that she knew I was on my way.

Just then the driver came up the aisle collecting fares before he started the journey. I brought out twelve hryvnia, remembering the cost from two days before. When I gave him the money he said something to me and waited. I didn't know what the problem was but just then the lady behind came forward and sat beside me. She handed the driver two hryvnia on my behalf. I later discovered that the fare could vary depending on the bus company.

I attempted to have a conversation with this kind lady as we sat together for the trip, which was extended due to a road closure. The diversion through a darkened forest road added a further forty minutes onto our journey. She told me her name was Galina and she lived on the outskirts of Malin with her family. I was able to tell her a little about my own family, although the conversation was painfully slow due to the language barrier. I asked where she worked but I didn't understand her reply. She brought a piece of paper from her handbag with writing on it, but I couldn't read the words. So then Galina reached into her shopping bag and pulled out a paper bag of doughnuts. She pointed at it and said in Russian, "I work here." As she offered me a doughnut I realised Galina worked in a bakery. I was hungry and it tasted great. Before she got off the bus she insisted I take another doughnut and also made sure I knew at which stop to disembark.

I came off the bus at the correct place but as I wandered round the town square it dawned on me that I had no idea how to make it to the hospital, which is located on the fringes of Malin. There were buses waiting on both sides of the road but I didn't know which of the coaches would take me to my destination. I stopped passers-by, saying "vrach, vrach", Russian for "doctor, doctor", and pointed in what I thought was the general direction of the hospital, but no one could understand what I wanted.

I saw a taxi approaching, so flagged that down in the hope I might have more luck. The Lada with its typically cracked windscreen came to a halt and the driver rolled down his window. I attempted some mime, pretending to attach a stethoscope to my ears and holding it against my chest. I repeated this performance and pointed again in the direction of the hospital, saying, "vrach, diety (children)".

He nodded and indicated for me to climb inside. Now I just had to trust that he understood. After a few minutes I recognised the road and the hospital came into sight. As he pulled up outside I thanked him and said, "skolka stoit?"

I didn't understand his response so I brought some money from my pocket and placed it on my palm. He lifted some notes, about the equivalent of £1.50, and drove away. I trudged up the stairs with my bag, finally making it to the children's ward, albeit several hours late.

The incident reinforced two points: I struggled to travel in Ukraine on my own but thankfully the people are very helpful and friendly.

Not too long after this episode I was travelling solo on the Kiev metro again when I decided to come off at the station one before my usual stop, so that I could walk to Maidan square. When I reached the exits I realised there were three options. While I dithered over which one to choose I heard a voice behind me say in English, "Can I help you?"

I turned round and saw a lovely, well dressed woman. Trying to regain my composure I replied, "You speak English".

"Of course."

"But how did you know I was a foreigner?"

"You looked lost," she laughed.

"You're right about that," I smiled. "I'm trying to find my way to Maidan square from here. Can you help me?"

"Of course," she replied, and we set off. I asked if she had time for a coffee and she told me she had no plans for the afternoon, so we went to a nearby restaurant and had a good chat.

Her name was Alla Knyzhanorska and her husband was a Ukrainian diplomat in Canada. She later took me on a tour of the city to many places I had never seen, such as the underground church, a fascinating place. When it was time to meet Anatoli I introduced him to Alla and suggested that we, along with Anatoli's wife Elena, go out for dinner. Two nights later we ate at O'Pana's, a restaurant on the edge of Shevchenko Park that Elena had always wished to visit. In the park on the way I saw ice sculptors working, which was fantastic to watch, and inside the restaurant two young ladies entertained us by playing a traditional Ukrainian musical instrument called a bandura, a large lute-like instrument with thirty-eight strings and a terrifically melodious sound. At the end of the night we walked Alla to her apartment block, where outside a guard presence was visible due to the building being used by diplomats and their families. I was glad Alla had introduced herself in the Metro station. She was a very nice and interesting woman, and the four of us had a good night together.

These are just a selection of the adventures and encounters while visiting Ukraine. There have been many more and hopefully plenty still to come, but one thing is for sure: a trip to my adopted country will never be uneventful.

And I wouldn't want it any other way.

Transport Adventures

When I first set out on my ventures to Ukraine I made the decision to travel on land for two reasons.

The first was the cost; any money raised or donated goes to the children in Malin. I do not use a penny of it to pay for my transportation. That hasn't always been easy and in some years I have struggled, but with Margaret's help and understanding I have managed to pay my own way.

Secondly I realised that – even prior to 9/11 – I would have great difficulty trying to take medical supplies through airport customs, not to mention the cost of extra baggage. The bus posed fewer problems, where my only limitation was how much I could physically carry.

Many people find it hard to envisage sitting on a cramped bus with only occasional stops for three days at a time. It isn't the most pleasant mode of travel, I concede, but I have never felt stir crazy. Maybe that's because I know the end result is worth it – whether it's helping the hospital or, on the return trip, seeing my family.

I am often asked how I occupy those long hours.

Well, there are often movies shown on the buses. These are usually in Russian language with Ukrainian or Polish subtitles, but if it is a film I have already seen then I can follow the plot.

What I try to do most of all, though, is talk with my fellow passengers. I like meeting new people and it helps me to improve and practice my Russian. And if I am failing to make myself understood I bring out some of the Ukrainian newspaper cuttings that have featured me over the years and I'll show these to my new companions to explain why I'm travelling across Europe from Scotland. It's a good conversation starter.

I remember the year I came home via Antwerp on the bus. We had time to kill before the connecting bus left, so I went to a local cafe with three Russian women who were passengers on my coach. The lady working in the cafe could speak a little English, so I acted as the conduit between the two parties. The three women told me in Russian that they wanted bread, tea and coffee and I translated the order to the waitress in English.

Later on that same trip, as we left the Belgian city, I befriended a couple of Russian ladies who were eating meat and drinking vodka to while away the hours. They insisted I have some of their food and drink and we spent the rest of the night having a good laugh and chat. The following morning, when the bus had stopped, I saw the younger of the two women looking the worse for wear when I went out to stretch my legs. I think maybe she had over indulged on the vodka the night before and was paying the price, although she managed to raise a little smile when she saw me looking at her.

The bus journeys are not without incident. Far from it. Over the years I have been witness to scary border checks, delays, diversions and breakdowns, and been subjected to robberies, missed buses, culture clashes and so much more.

I had been dozing intermittently when I realised we were pulling into the bus station in Brussels city centre. I thought time must have crept away from me while I snoozed but a look at my watch showed it was only around 3.30am – the bus hadn't been due to arrive until six am. Brussels was the coach's final destination (I often booked whatever route was the cheapest) and a connecting bus was to depart the station at 6.30am to London. Had the bus been on time I expected not to have long to wait.

Here I was though, more than two hours early, being ushered off the vehicle half sleeping in the middle of a cold night and into a deserted station. As everyone shuffled off it became clear that nobody was waiting around. Brussels appeared to be the final destination for my fellow passengers and soon I was all alone in the vast station.

With my bags in tow I tiredly wandered round the depot, which had an adjoining train station. I came across a waiting room but it was locked. I leaned against the wall of the building, hoping that the overhang from the roof would shelter me from the biting cold. My hands were tingling.

The depot appeared to be in the city centre, so I decided to take a walk to try to find somewhere still open where I could sit in the warmth until it was time to come back for the London connection. Before setting off I checked the studs on jacket pocket were fastened. My tickets and digital camera were inside and I was paranoid about losing them. It was my first digital camera. My family had bought it for me just a few months before and I'd taken a lot of pictures at the hospital. I turned out of the depot and walked up a deserted street, hoping to encounter some signs of civilisation.

After a moment or two I spotted someone approaching me in the distance. As the person came closer I realised it was a lady or, more aptly when I saw what she was wearing, a lady of the night. This was not the sort of civilisation I had in mind. She said something to me and although I didn't understand the words I had a fair idea of what she was proposing, so I made my way past her as swiftly as I could.

It was a relatively short walk to the main drag of the city but it unfortunately everywhere was closed. There was no point drifting aimlessly around the rows of shuttered shops and darkened cafes, so I decided to go back to the depot. Hopefully the waiting area might soon open.

It was around five am when I returned to the station. I was relieved to see there were a couple of people now sitting in the waiting room, so I joined them. I sat down in a plastic seat, glad to be in from the cold but very tired. My jacket was fastened up to my chin and I could feel the camera tight against my body in my pocket as my eyes began to close.

I don't know how long I had been sleeping before I was wakened with a start. Someone was shaking my shoulder and I looked up to see a man standing over me. I was quite alarmed. He pressed the palms of his hands together and placed them by the side of his head in a sleeping motion. 'Security' was the only word he said that I recognised. I stood up and attempted to explain I was waiting on a bus, that I wasn't a drifter just using the place to sleep.

He moved alongside me and motioned with his hands as if he were clutching a steering wheel. Then he moved his legs up and down and began jumping. I looked around but by now we were the only two people in the room. He was not acting in an aggressive way but his manner was unsettling. After wandering the city for so long there was no way I was going back outside until my bus was due, and I told him that, but whether or not he understood was debatable.

He continued jumping around, even bumping into me at one point, until he stopped and held up five fingers. I took this to mean five minutes and as he left the waiting room I wondered if he was going to return in five minutes or if that was how long he was giving me to get out of there.

My heart was thumping and I was a little shaken at being wakened in an unfamiliar city with a stranger standing over me. Especially one who was acting in such a peculiar fashion. I rubbed my sweaty hands down the front of my jacket and it was then that I noticed the bulge of my camera was missing.

I looked down, panicked, and saw the two studs on my pocket were open. Immediately I thought of all the pictures I had taken in Malin. I presumed this so-called security guard (he wore dark clothing but no uniform) must have snatched it while he distracted me with all that movement and strange behaviour.

I rushed outside to look for him but he was nowhere to be seen. I went over to the railway station to check if anyone there could help. A door was opened but I couldn't locate any staff. I didn't know how to call the police, so I consigned myself to going back to the waiting room where I would just have to wait for the Euroline office to open before I could report the theft.

At approximately 5.55am Euroline's doors were unlocked. The man behind the desk confirmed he spoke English, so I explained what had happened. He told me I needed to report it to the police.

"Can't you do it on my behalf?" I asked.

"No, you must go to the police station and do it yourself."

I explained I was due to depart in half an hour, so I didn't have time to file a report it without fear of missing my bus. That was the last thing I needed after the morning I'd endured so far. I knew the theft had to reported for insurance purposes, so he agreed to write a note stating I had notified the bus company.

My coach departed on time and I forlornly made the journey back to Britain. When I arrived in London I went to Victoria police station and attempted to report the robbery, but they said since it didn't happen in London and because I didn't live there, nothing could be done about it from their side. What a complete nightmare.

When I returned home I contacted my insurance company. Eventually they paid out £135, which I put straight into the hospital fund, but there was no way of compensating for the lost pictures. At the time I worked with Royal Mail in Glasgow city centre. The staff knew of my trips and often held fundraising events in my honour, which I greatly appreciated. Word soon spread of the camera theft and my kind co-workers presented me with a Canon, which I have used on my visits ever since.

I'm relieved to say this incident is the only time I have been robbed during my trips to Ukraine. The only other attempt, to my knowledge, was the first trip during that incident in Warsaw as I climbed onto the tram.

But that incident in the early hours of Brussels was enough to make me stay alert in the future. Now I always ensure my camera is hidden well away from any roaming hands.

Usually I arrive and depart from the bus station in central Kiev, but in 2002 my return ticket instructed I should leave from a station in the city's suburbs. Anatoli drove me in his minivan and on the way we passed by a fire station. Firefighters were in the news at home at the time due to a proposed strike over a pay dispute, and I told Anatoli I would be interested to see the inner workings of the Ukrainian fire service.

No sooner had the words passed my lips than Anatoli was cutting across the road and parking outside the station. He told me to wait a moment while he went inside and spoke to the firefighters. A few minutes later Anatoli returned to the van and said to come with him.

We went inside, where I was introduced to some of the firemen, who were dressed in military-like garbs, and shown around. I could not believe how antiquated the fire engines looked. In Britain the Green Goddesses were being prepared by the military in case the strikes came to fruition, but the vehicles being utilised everyday in Ukraine appeared as equally old-fashioned, if not more so.

With Anatoli translating I chatted with the men, who failed to comprehend how the British fire service could even be allowed to strike. It just would not happen in Ukraine. They offered to take me on a ride in one of their fire engines but as much as I would have liked to take up their offer, the time was ticking until my bus was due to leave. We said our goodbyes, returned to the van and made our way to the unfamiliar bus station.

We passed through a residential area and by a main street with a few shops before turning into the sprawling station. Anatoli was due to start work soon, so he asked if I would be okay to wait by myself. I was in the right place with plenty of time before the bus was due, so I told him I would be fine.

I lifted my bag and waved goodbye to my friend for another year, and then made my way into the main concourse of the station. I stood in front of the long, narrow administrative building that contained the ticket office and toilets and looked out across the forecourt.

There were local buses coming in and out regularly - decrepit, noisy vehicles that wheezed great big puffs of black smoke from their exhausts. Over on the opposite side were a number of buses that had long since given up the fight and were being left to rot within the confines of the busy depot.

I wasn't sure where I should be waiting, so at first I just stood and watched the buses coming in, hoping to spot an Eastern European Travel company's vehicle sporting the London destination board. When this failed to materialise, I checked along all the bus stops for any notification of where the long distance journeys might usually depart, but without success.

I was beginning to worry because it was fast approaching the departure time. I went inside to the ticket booth but unfortunately the woman on the opposite side of the glass didn't understand English. In my very limited Russian I tried to ask where I should wait for the London bus, but she didn't know what I was saying. I brought the ticket from my pocket and held it up. She signalled for me to pass it through and she disappeared into an office with it. My heart skipped a beat as I wondered whether or not she would return with my ticket. A minute later she reappeared and slid it back to me. She said something incomprehensible; the only word I recognised was pravda, correct, and then she smiled and looked to the next person in the line.

I really had no idea what to do. I was growing increasingly anxious because I had no way of communicating with the people around me, I had no mobile to call anyone for help and I didn't even know where I was.

I went back outside and scanned the parked buses; in amongst the local destinations was one bound for Germany, but London remained elusive. While I stood in the busy concourse with people brushing by me from every angle as they hurried to and from buses, I spotted an elderly man and woman stood together deep in conversation. They were each holding a carrier bag and it appeared some sort of deal was being made. For a moment I forgot my dilemma and focussed on the pair, but rather than being witness to an unlawful exchange I saw that what they were trading was perfectly legal, although somewhat bizarre. From his bag the old man brought out an empty plastic two-litre drinks bottle. In a swap the woman gave him two smaller plastic bottles, and with that they parted ways. I've no idea why they would meet to exchange such worthless items, but they seemed quite happy with the transaction.

As the lady passed by me I tapped her on the arm and offered her some of the toffees I had in my pocket. She took four and looked very pleased as she walked away.

But this was all just a distraction. My bus was now thirty minutes overdue and I was beginning to fear the worst – that I had missed my pick-up. With no sign of the coach in the terminal I decided to take a walk round the block on the off chance that I happened to see someone who could help.

I took a right at the end of the administrative building and headed towards the junction of the main street, where I could see a number of shops in the distance. In my line of sight I noticed a man walking towards me. I thought I recognised him, and at that moment he began waving.

It was the bus driver!

Three drivers share the duties on the long journey and I remembered him from the way over.

For a reason I didn't grasp, the bus was leaving from the main road rather than the station. Thankfully he had waited and after a while decided to come and look for me. I was glad he did. Finally I made it onto the bus and the long journey home to Cumbernauld could commence.

Then there was the time I was almost stranded at a German service station. The bus driver had stopped at what was, in comparison to others, a rather nice rest stop. I located a phone box to call Margaret, since I didn't have a mobile at this point.

Thankfully I could see the bus from the callbox, because while I was chatting I saw my coach slowly moving off. With barely a word of explanation to my wife I hung up the phone and rushed after the vehicle as it passed by. I ran alongside it and banged on the windows as the surprised passengers looked down. Mercifully the vehicle slowed down and the door opened.

"On you come," said the driver nonchalantly. I returned to my seat, breathless and rather flustered. I had narrowly avoided being stranded in Germany with no phone, currency or knowledge of the language. From that moment on, every time a bus driver stops for a break, I make sure to ask how long before he sets off again. Every experience is a lesson learned!

It's not just in foreign countries I experience travelling difficulties. One of my more recent trips was almost over before it started and it was completely my fault.

I checked over my luggage at my Cumbernauld home, just before I left to catch the 11.30pm National Express overnight coach to London. My good friend Eddie had offered to drive me to Buchanan Bus Station and we left around 10.30pm to ensure we allowed for any unforeseen delays giving ourselves plenty of time to get there. I gave Margaret a kiss and cuddle and told her I would call when I arrived in London.

The roads were quiet so we arrived early. Eddie dropped me off to the rear of the station and I carried my bags round to the main concourse, keeping a lookout for the bus as I walked. I was surprised to see it hadn't arrived yet, since it was due to leave in thirty minutes. I approached a bus station worker and asked if he knew where the London bus was.

"It's gone," he replied. "It left at 10.30pm."

"No, that's not right. It's not due to leave until 11.30pm." While I was speaking I pulled the ticket out from my coat pocket.

"Oh no," I muttered. I had been so sure of the time I hadn't even checked the ticket beforehand. I immediately realised my mistake – National Express's bus from London to Glasgow leaves at 11.30pm, but from Glasgow to London it departs at 10.30pm.

"I need to be in London tomorrow morning to catch another bus," I explained in a panic.

He told me there were no other buses due to leave for the capital but a sleeper train departed Glasgow Central, although he didn't know its departure time. Central was no more than a swift ten-minute walk from the bus station but I didn't know how long I had to spare, so I rushed to the taxi rank and jumped in a cab. I made it to the train station within a couple of minutes and I rushed to the ticket booth. The London train wasn't due to depart until 11.45pm. I hadn't missed it! Now I just had to hope there were seats available. I was told there was a berth left, but it cost £62. The bus fare had only been £12 but there was nothing else for it; I had to pay the fee if I wanted to be in London by the morning.

After buying the ticket and finding the correct platform, I gave Margaret a call.

"Why aren't you on the bus?" she asked, hearing the noise of the station in the background.

"I decided to take the train for a change," I responded, before confessing what really happened.

"How much did that cost?"

"Well, it was more than the bus."

It was a costly lesson but had I not caught the train it would have brought even bigger problems. Now I always double-check my tickets before travelling, no matter how many times I might have made the journey.

It was the third and final day on the cramped bus when the driver pulled into the station at Rivne. Although we were on the home stretch there were still two hundred miles to drive before we reached Kiev. Rivne is a historic city in Western Ukraine and an important transportation hub in the country. Not only does it have rail links to Zdolbiniv, Sarny and Kovel, and highways connecting it to Brest, Kiev and Lviv, but it's also home to an international airport. But for me it was the bus. The driver pulled into a concrete bay, where there were one or two people waiting to board. For some passengers Rivne was their final destination. For me, it was the ideal time for a toilet break. I stepped gingerly off the bus, my bones aching from being cooped up, and emerged into the dimly lit station.

I walked towards the back of the station, where there were

offices, a couple of shops and the bathroom. The toilets were really grotty and terribly smelly.

As I walked back to the bus I could see two young girls standing by the door. They were young, the eldest no older than ten years old and the other, who looked to be her sister, maybe around seven. It was ten pm, so I wondered why they were there alone.

The two girls said something to me. It was the same phrase they repeated over and over, words I recognised. Money, please. Money, please. The girls were wearing winter coats and didn't look like they were orphaned or homeless, but why else would they be standing in a dark bus station begging for money on a cold winter's night?

I motioned for them to wait a moment while I went inside the bus to collect a packet of biscuits I had in my bag. But they declined my offer of food and repeated again that they wanted money.

Just as this was happening a woman coming off the bus warned me against giving the kids any cash. She told me it was likely that their parents had sent them out of the house to beg in order to bring home money.

As the bus reversed out of the bay I watched the girls standing together shivering. I felt so bad sitting in the warm vehicle while they roamed the dark streets, begging for money under instruction of their parents. I wished my language skills were better, so I could have at least talked to the girls. But then again, what good would it have done?

I watched the girls until they faded into the darkness and we drove on to Kiev, nearer to a place where I could at least try to help some needy children.

Crossing borders can quite often be a fearful and anxious experience, especially the Polish-Ukrainian border. It's easy to tell when we're approaching the border, because there are several kilometres of parked lorries waiting to be checked before they are allowed to proceed. The crossing guards are very thorough – I've even seen them checking in the exhaust pipes.

It can be quite an ordeal just for a bus and its passengers to make it into Ukraine, too. Sometimes the guards order everyone off the vehicle and make us put our luggage on a conveyor to be checked. They order each passenger forward one at a time and look at our passports. Only when they are satisfied will they allow the people and their possessions to return to the bus. On other occasions I've seen the guards come on and study each individual's passport. They stare at the picture and then the person for what feels like an eternity. Occasionally they take the passport away to run checks and I always wonder if they'll return flanked with extra security.

One time a man was frogmarched off the bus. Maybe he had the wrong papers or there were discrepancies with his passport, but he never came back. Even though I had no reason to fear such a scenario, I slid down in my seat at the back of the bus wondering if the same fate might befall me. It's quite a disturbing sight to see, like a scene from a Cold War spy movie. Thankfully I've never had a problem at border checks, and I hope that remains the case in the future.

Sometimes just making it to the border checks is a triumph, because the buses threaten to expire before we can make it that far.

The bus had been driving along miles of darkened road in the dead of night when I first noticed the smell. It was quite pungent but I wasn't sure it was coming from our vehicle. But after a few minutes I had no doubt and it was obviously noted by the driver too, because soon after he pulled over.

The three drivers on board went out into the early morning chill to investigate the rather worrying odour. I later discovered they had found some exposed wiring in the luggage hold that had caught fire and it was this that created the smell. They simply threw some water over the wires and were on the road again soon afterwards. Not technical but it seemed to be effective.

I wasn't so lucky on other time I'd been on the Eastern European Travel bus from London. We were now driving through Poland and I was sitting near the back of the bus at the kerbside when I began to hear this rhythmic boom, boom, boom noise. At first, I wasn't sure what was making the racket. Maybe it was from a fellow passenger's headphones or roadworks further down the road. But as the sound continued I realised it was coming from the bus and, specifically, the area where I sat.

Soon the bus was parked and the three drivers were gathered round the wheel below my feet. They spent some time deliberating and poking around at the tyre, before coming back on and restarting the engine. We moved off slowly and continued at that snail-like pace as we drove into the historical Lublin, the biggest city in the east of Poland.

It was early in the morning, around six am, and the streets of the city were still quiet. We turned into a narrow side street and I wondered where we were going. This was not the usual route. As we crept downhill there was suddenly a bang, a huge explosion, from under the bus. We jumped in our seats. Some people were awakened with a fright, other passengers gasping or yelping in shock.

The bus came to a halt once again and the drivers went back out. Soon we were on the move again, still going slowly, until we pulled into a Volvo garage. Those passengers who hadn't already been roused were shook awake by the drivers, who instructed us to get off.

We were told that one of the tyres at the rear of the vehicle had blown out and we had come to this Volvo dealership, which was luckily nearby, to have it repaired. Here we were, many of the passengers still groggy, in a Polish garage in the morning darkness. And here we remained for several hours while we waited for the problem to be fixed.

I wandered round the large yard surrounding the garage, passing by rows of lorries and buses, some waiting to be repaired, others beyond repair. I spotted something red that caught my eye in amongst the vehicles. I moved in for a closer look and was rather surprised to see an old-style British fire engine. There was a Russian man working on it and I managed to conduct a short conversation with him. He told me that the vehicles are transported to Eastern Europe once they've been deleted by the UK fire service. They're converted to left-hand drive and then put back into operation in a new country.

When I returned to the garage I saw the huge break drum had been removed from our bus. The bearings had seized up, causing the heat to build and the tyre to subsequently explode.

It was clear we were going to be stuck here for a while, so I called Anatoli from my mobile. He was supposed to be picking me up when I arrived in Kiev, but when I explained the situation he said he would no longer be able, because he had to go to work. He told me to hail a taxi instead, and to call him so he could speak to the driver and give him directions to his home.

We were stuck at the garage for several hours before getting back on our way. It was late before I finally arrived at my friend's house in a taxi.

On my earlier trips, before I discovered the Kiev to London bus, I would take the train from Kiev to Warsaw on my way home, followed by the bus from Warsaw to London. The visit had not run entirely smoothly on this visit because I hadn't realised that my credit card had expired prior to the journey. This created a few problems. I had spent all of my cash by the trip's end and as I entered Warsaw bus station all I had in my wallet was a Scottish five pound note.

It was OK because I had my ticket for the bus already, although it would have been nice to have bought some food and drink for the journey.

But while I waited for my bus I learned that the ticket did not guarantee a seat. In a rather strange system, a deposit had to be paid at the bus station to reserve a space, in addition to the ticket.

I went to the ticket office and tried to explain to the lady that I had no Polish currency to pay the deposit. She could speak a little English and advised me there was a currency exchange within the station that would convert British money. I located the bureau de change and slid the fiver across to the man on the other side of the glass.

I watched uneasily as he studied the note. He held it to the light, examined it again and then pushed it back towards me, shaking his head. I explained it was Sterling but he refused to exchange the note. I could only presume this was because it was Scottish rather than English.

I went back to the woman in the ticket office and explained

what had happened. She said I would just have to wait to see if there was any space on the bus.

When the coach came in I looked nervously at the long queue forming by the door. I went over to the bag courier, who spoke English, and explained my situation. He told me to stand aside until he could determine how many passengers were coming on, and what felt like a never-ending line of people climbed aboard the bus while I anxiously waited. Finally the courier beckoned me and said there was space. I breathed a sigh of relief and bounded up the steps and found an empty seat.

I survived on just a cup of coffee until I boarded the ferry from France, where thankfully they did accept my Scottish note and I was able to buy some breakfast before embarking on the final leg of my trek.

I had made it home safely once again, and as I looked back on the trials and tribulations of my journey, I wondered what adventures would in store for my next trip to Malin.

Epilogue

A month after I returned from my 2009 trip to Malin and just a few days before Christmas, the postman delivered to my home an official looking letter, the content of which left me open mouthed.

"Dear Mr Jim Gillies, I have pleasure in inviting you and your partner to a reception in the City Chambers hosted by the Lord Provost and Council of the City of Edinburgh. A medal awarded by the Ukrainian Government will be presented at the reception to the Friends of Ukraine Scottish Foundation for the work carried out in establishing links and cooperation between Scotland and Ukraine. Jim Gillies of Cumbernauld will also be presented with a medal for his fundraising activities and supply of equipment for the children's hospital at Malyn near Kyiv. The reception will be held in the City Chambers High Street, Edinburgh on 29th January 2010 between 6.00pm and 7.00pm, and I look forward to meeting you then. Yours sincerely, Vadyk Vakhrushev, Consul of Ukraine in Edinburgh."

I was speechless. I had never done any of the fundraising or aid trips for self-gratification and I had no idea any sort of reception partly in my honour was being planned. Once I overcame the surprise I felt quite proud, and also humbled, that my efforts to help the children of Malin were being recognised. It was a lovely and unexpected Christmas and birthday present, although I couldn't help but wonder who might have nominated me or decided I was worthy of the award. Margaret, my kids, my mum, and the rest of my family and friends were delighted for me and also shared in my feelings of pride.

I hired a kilt to add a Scottish touch to the proceedings and Margaret took the day off work to accompany me. We drove to nearby Croy railway station and caught the train to Edinburgh. Once in the capital we made our way to the City Chambers, where we were the first to arrive. We were shown into a large, grand room where a buffet was laid out. As more people filtered in I realised I could have invited more of my friends and family, but I'd believed it was a private ceremony. I had been attended many of the events organised by the Friends of Ukraine Scottish Foundation, which was based in Edinburgh, for several years, so I knew a number of its members as they filtered in. I was really happy to see that Debi Edward, the STV reporter who had accompanied me on a Malin trip, had come along for the presentation.

My nerves were jangling as the ceremony began. Steve Cardownie, the Deputy Leader of the City of Edinburgh Council, said a few words to the audience of around fifty about my work in Ukraine and then Vadyk Vakhrushev asked me to come forward and accept my award. He shook my hand and said he was pleased to present me with a medal and scroll on behalf of the Ukrainian Government for my work in Malin.

The large scroll was written in Ukrainian but I understood that it came from the Ukrainian Ministry of Foreign Affairs.

The magnificent looking gold medal is inscribed with Ukrainian text and the image of a building.

One day I plan on having them translated but I haven't actually told Anatoli, the man who I would most likely ask to transcribe the words, about my award, nor have I told the staff at the hospital. While I feel very honoured to have been recognised, I think the people who are truly deserving of a medal are the doctors. What they have to go through on a daily basis to try to help the youngsters makes them much more worthy of any award than I will ever be.

In January 2011 I celebrated my seventieth birthday. I have no plans to stop fundraising or making my annual trips to Ukraine but I know at some point in time it will come to an end. I understand how much the hospital has come to rely on me; it almost seems like I am all they have and I do worry about the future. I have spent so much time and effort trying to improve conditions for them and it is frustrating, draining and tiring when promises are broken, pleas are ignored, bureaucracy reigns and negativity seems to be the end result to all I attempt to do. But I will keep going.

I may be seventy now but in my mind I am ageless. So long as I can afford the travel fares and have something to give to the children I will continue going for as long as I am physically able.

Honestly, I don't know what I will do when the day comes when I have to end my trips. When I first started this I thought as time passed I would meet like-minded people and build a foundation of individuals who would carry on helping and visiting the hospital once I stopped. Unfortunately it hasn't worked out that way.

With that written, I have met many wonderful people both

in Ukraine and at home, and without the support and donations of the latter I wouldn't have been able to help the hospital as much as I have done.

I suppose I also held out hope that twenty-five years after Chernobyl the hospital might be moving out of poverty and wouldn't be so reliant on the help of a pensioner from Scotland, but as I explained earlier politics is a dirty game in Ukraine and the plight of present and future generations of the country's children is of little concern to the government, far less the president. The day when hospitals like the one in Malin has enough equipment and medicine to treat its children is, I'm sad to say, a long way off.

That means, for me, there is still much to do.

I readily admit I am soft hearted and can become quite emotional while in the hospital. Maybe it would be easier if I could remain detached, but for better or worse that is not the way I am.

I worry when I think of what will happen when I do stop going, but I suppose the staff and patients at the hospital will know that at least there was one person who cared about them, if only for a short time.

When the day finally comes that I can no longer do this I think my heart will break. But I hope my passion and commitment to the children of Malin hospital can drive me on to ensure that day remains a long way off.

I'm only one man, but good intentions and a willingness to help can go a long way. In my case, fifteen hundred miles.

From Glasgow to Chernobyl, with love.